To Joe
and Nancy
on your 1st
You are both so ha
love -- we are so ha
for you. When I saw
book I could not think
of a couple more in love,
+ a couple who more
deserves a lifetime
of "confetti moments"
Enjoy!
Love,
Donna + Matt
Fitzsimmons

TO

FROM

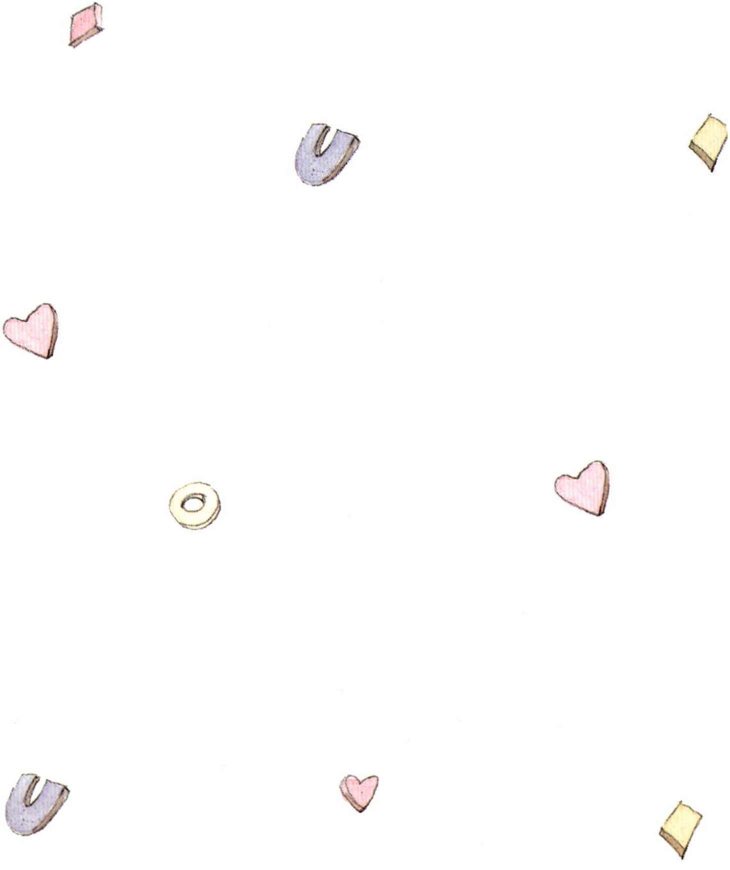

Little Dreams of Love

Illustrations by Julia Glynn Smith

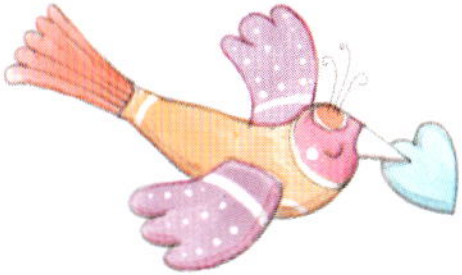

Andrews McMeel Publishing
Kansas City

Confetti Moments

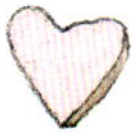

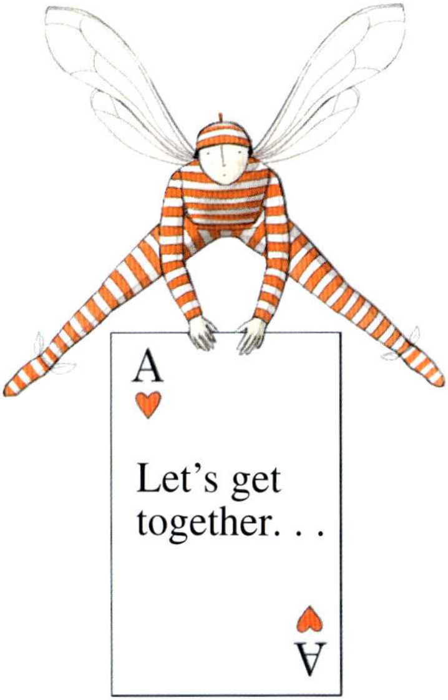
A
Let’s get together. . .
A

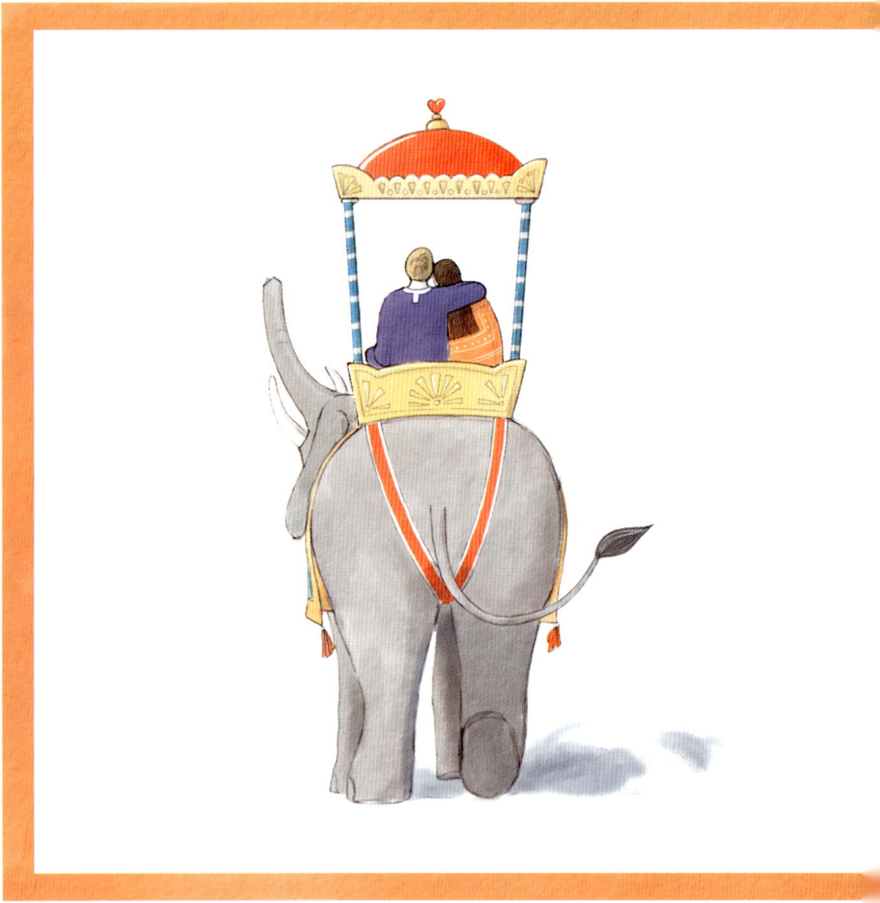

how wild and
wonderful being
carried away
by you

you and me . . .

magic together

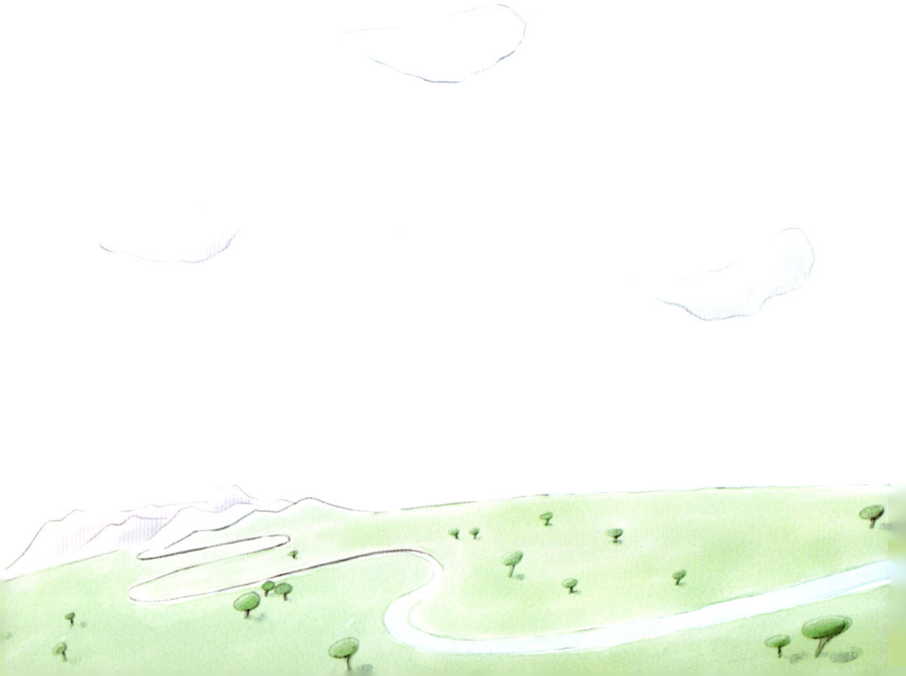

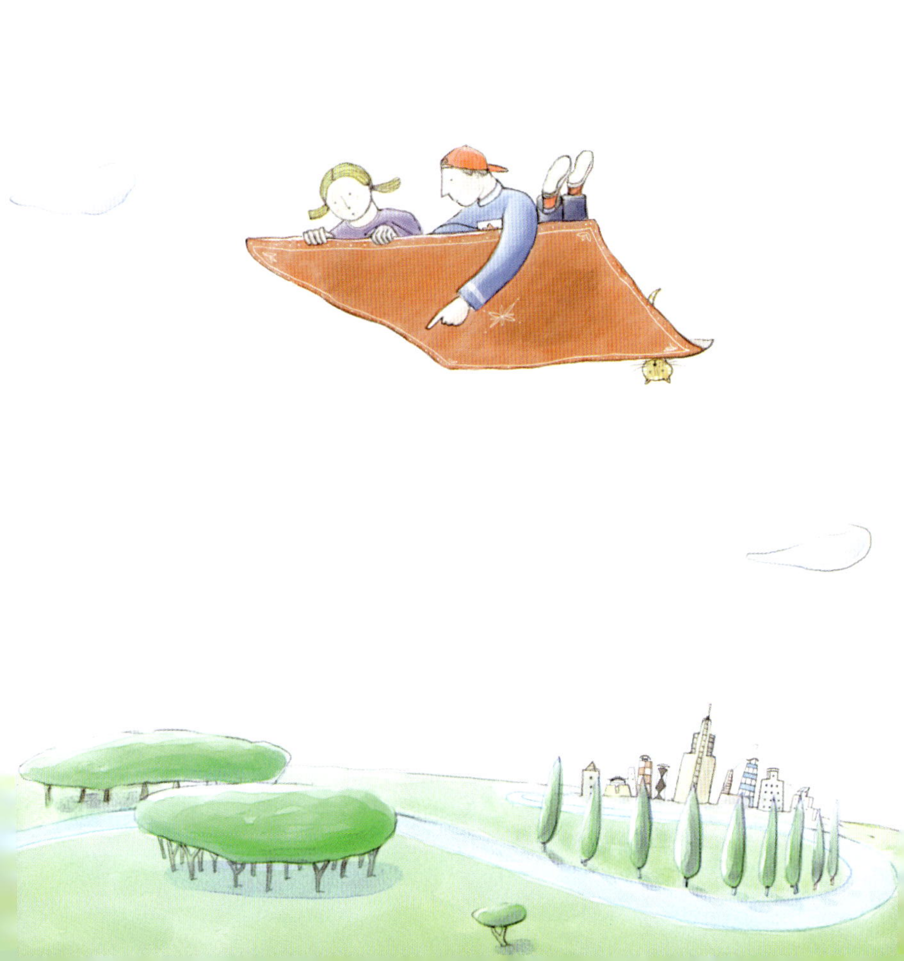

no matter where . . .

together with you

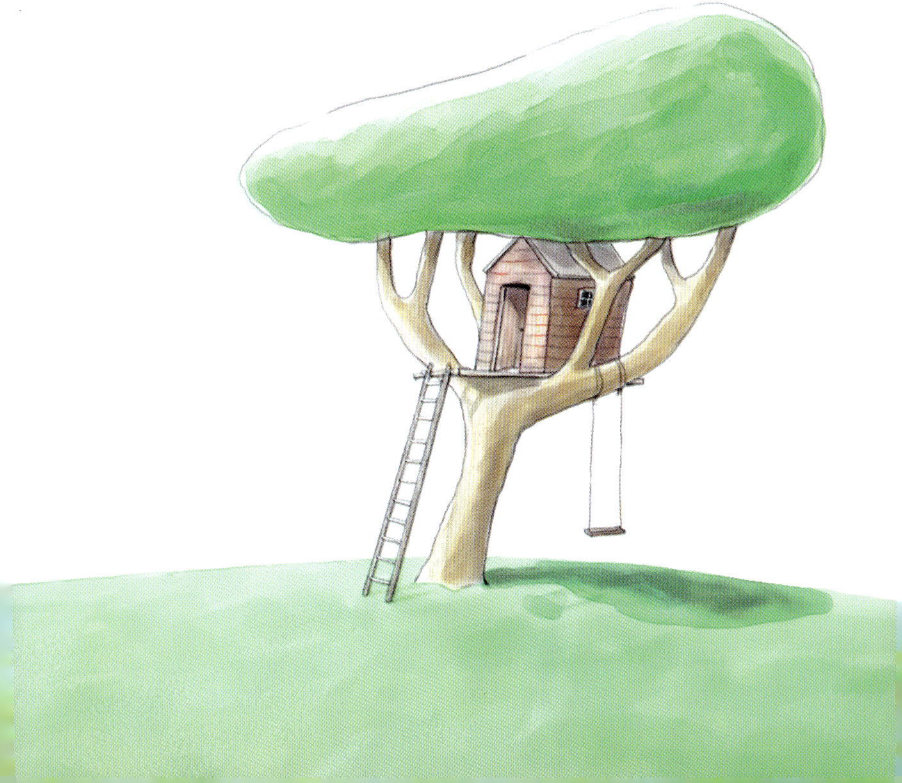

Confetti Moment

★ 1 ★

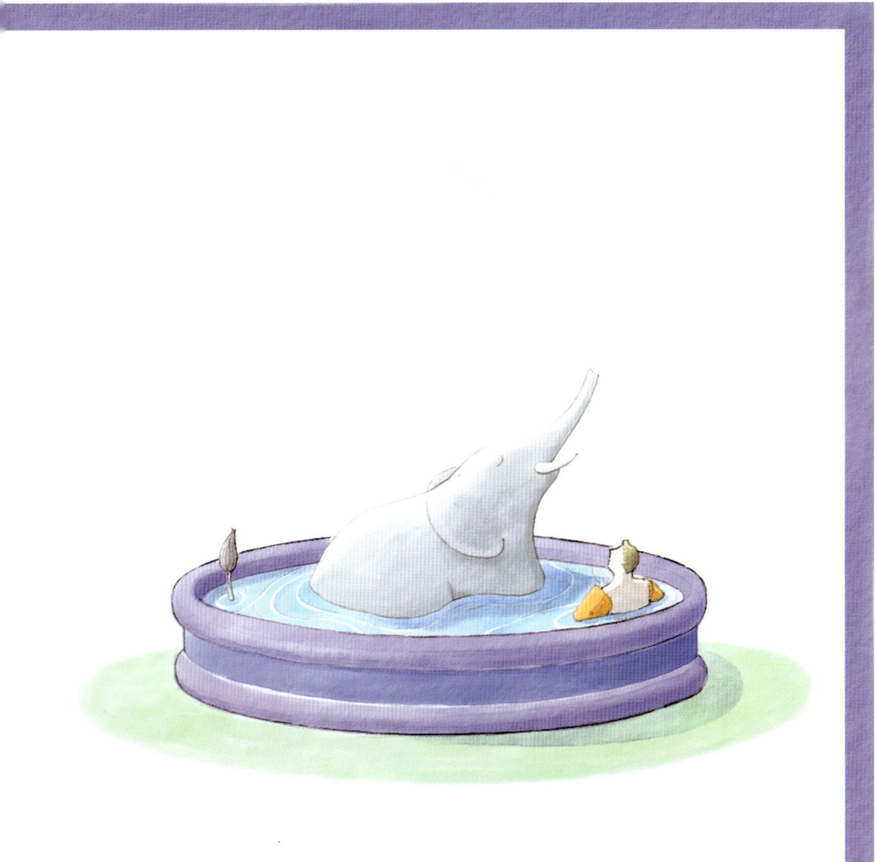

you're the one honeybee for me

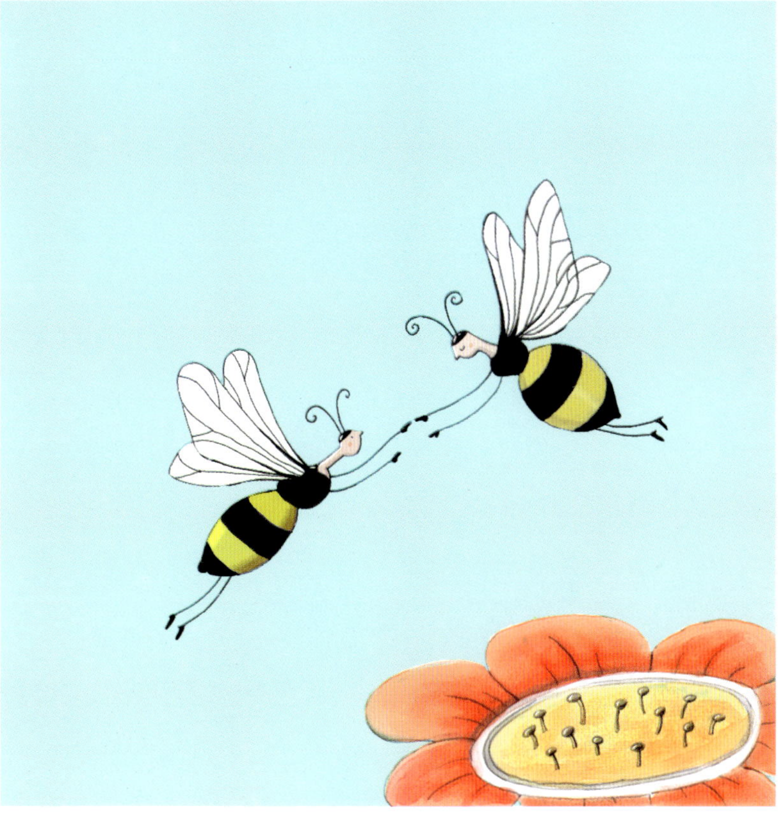

love multiplied

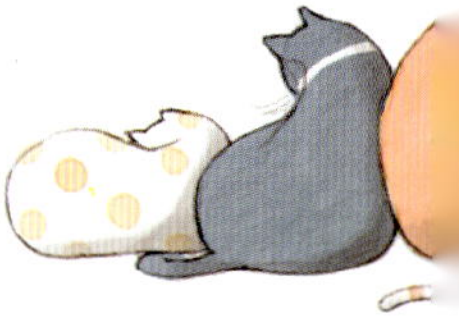

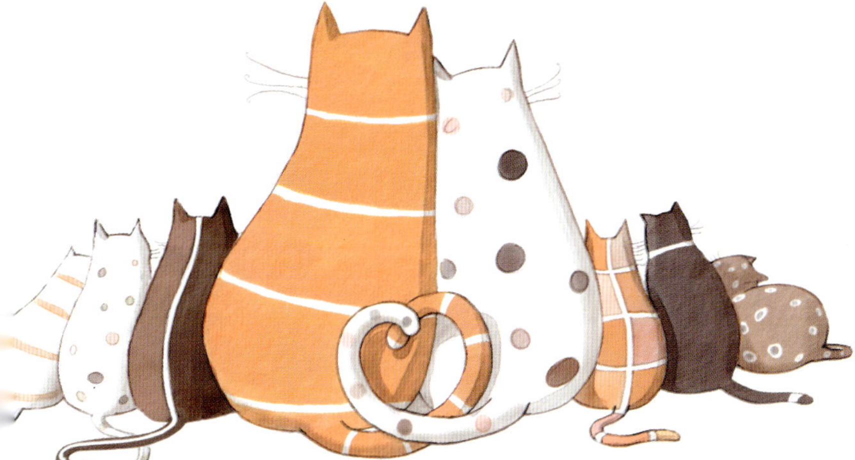

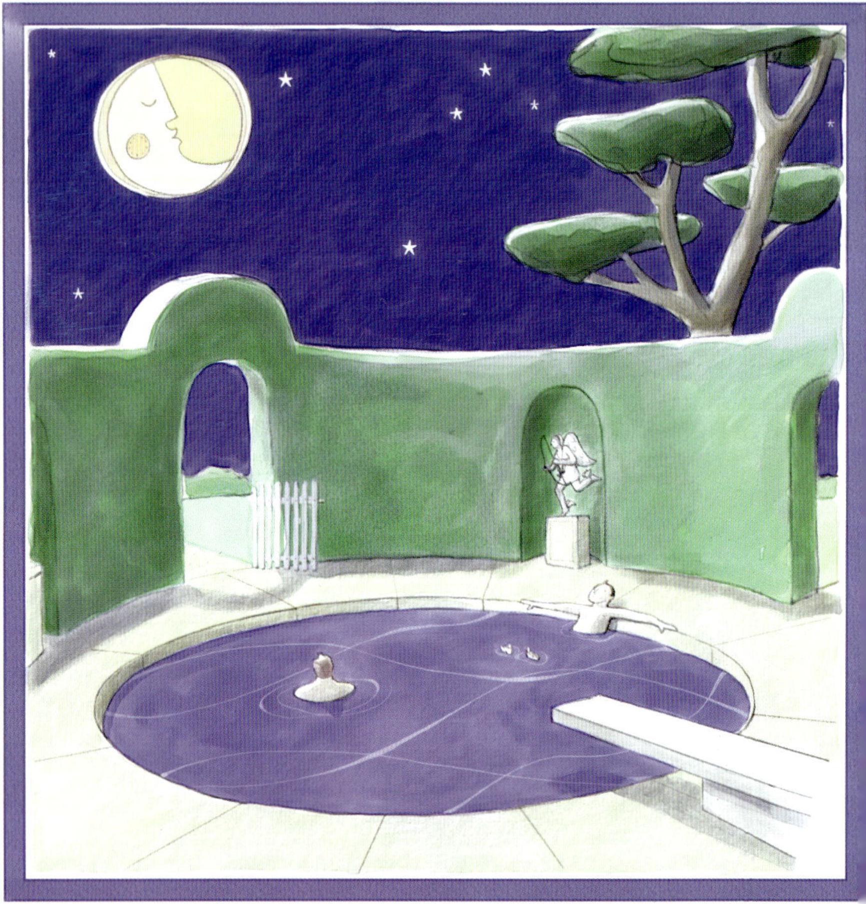

midnight in the silver-soft garden
is every night with you

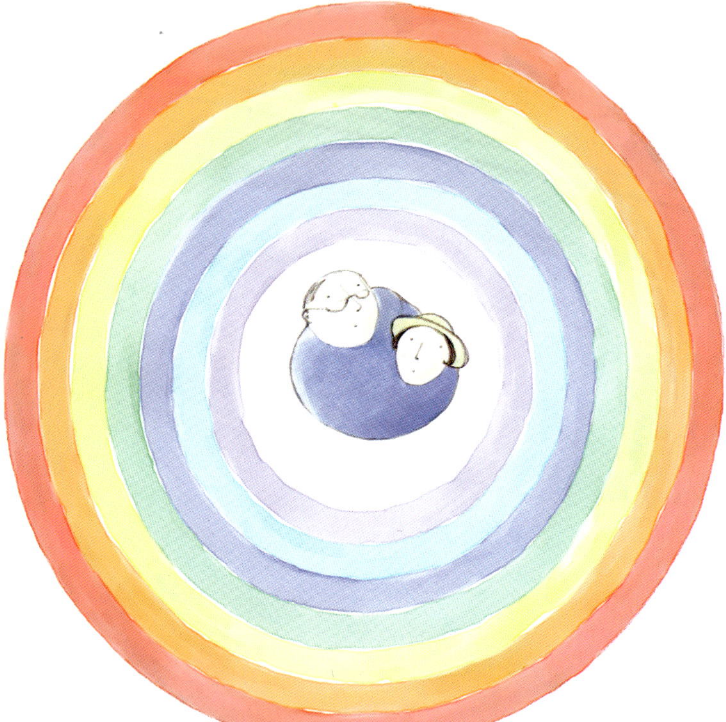

you and me
perfect happiness
and no end to
the rainbow

together...

into the sunset

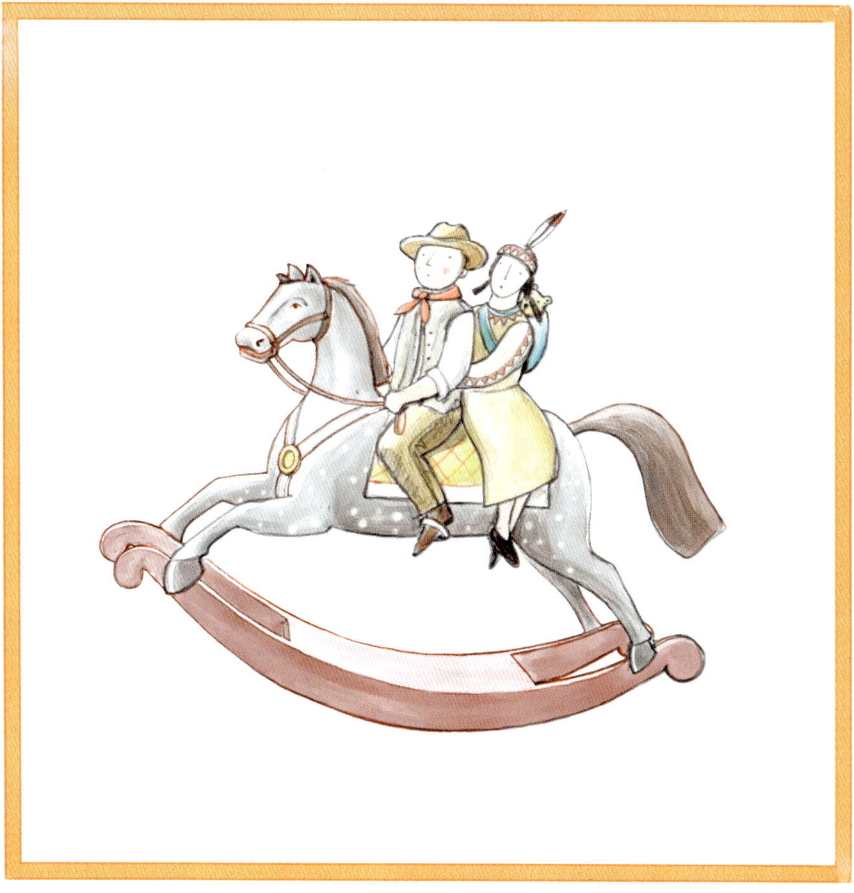

Confetti Moment

★ 2 ★

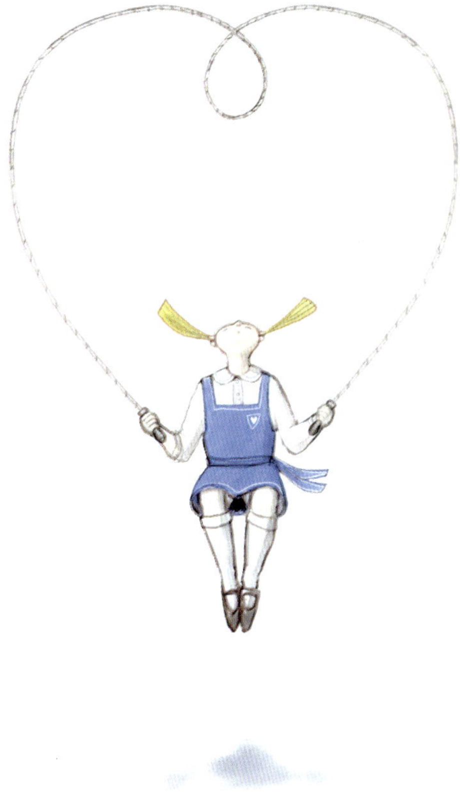

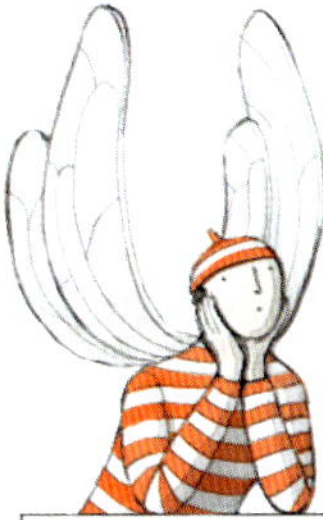

How sweet it is . . .

with you

anything is possible

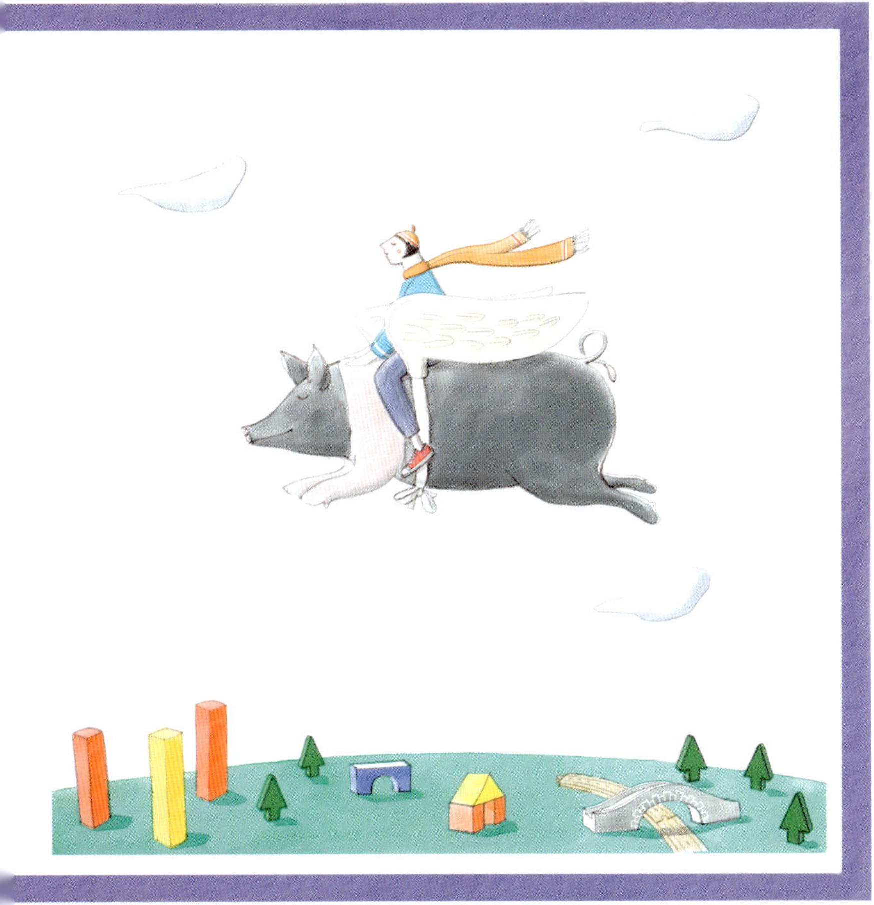

the thought of you

makes me cartwheel

and somersault

all the way

to your place

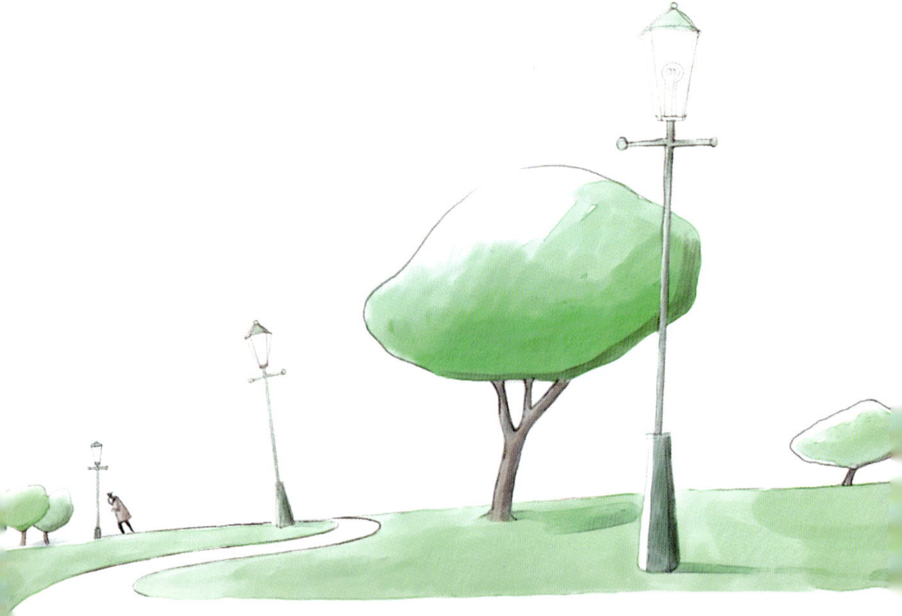

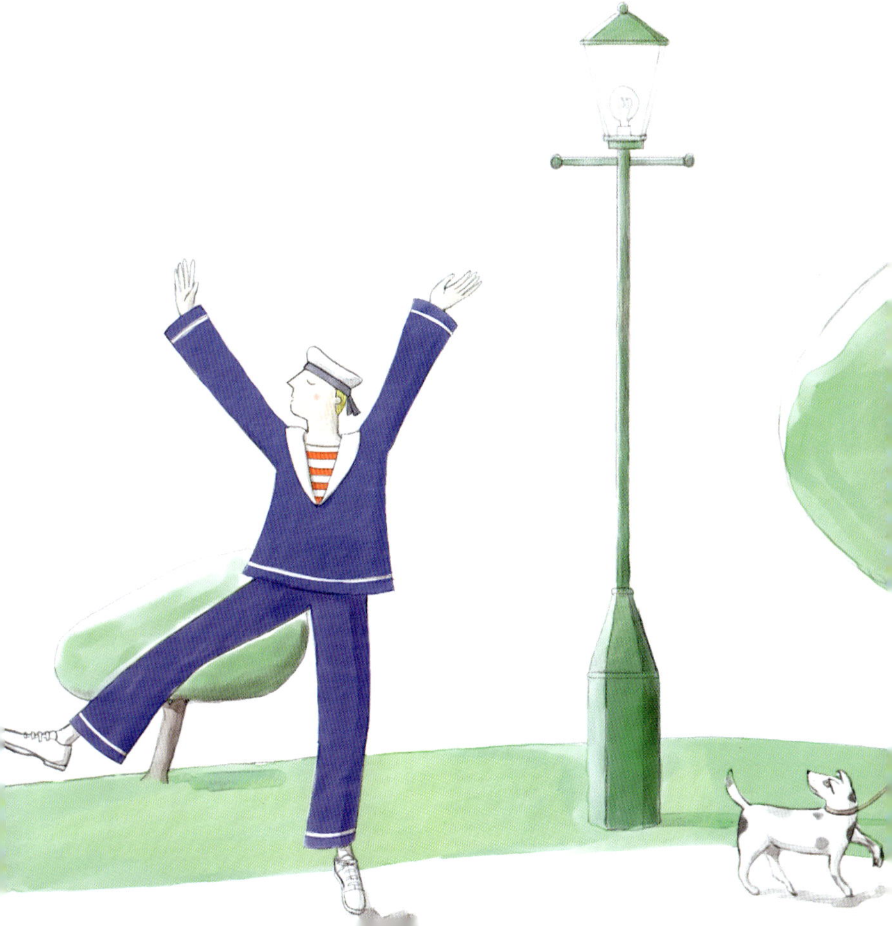

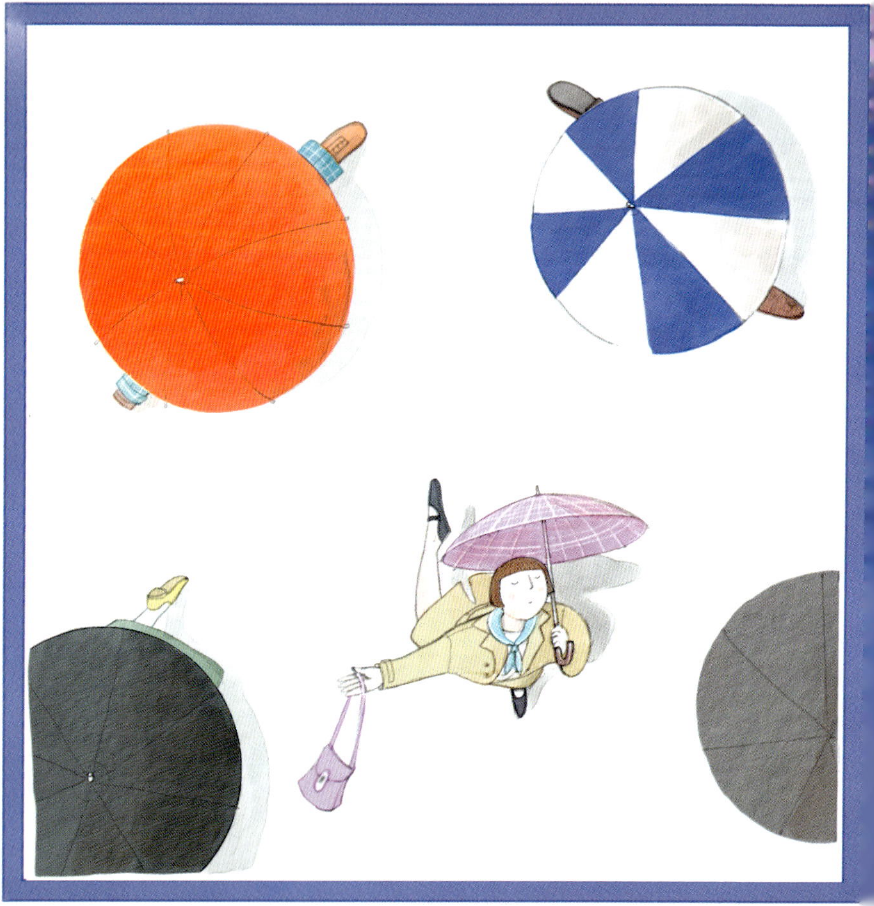

I could dance
in the rain or sun
on Mars or on Venus
just thinking
of you

CONFETTI MOMENT

★ 3 ★

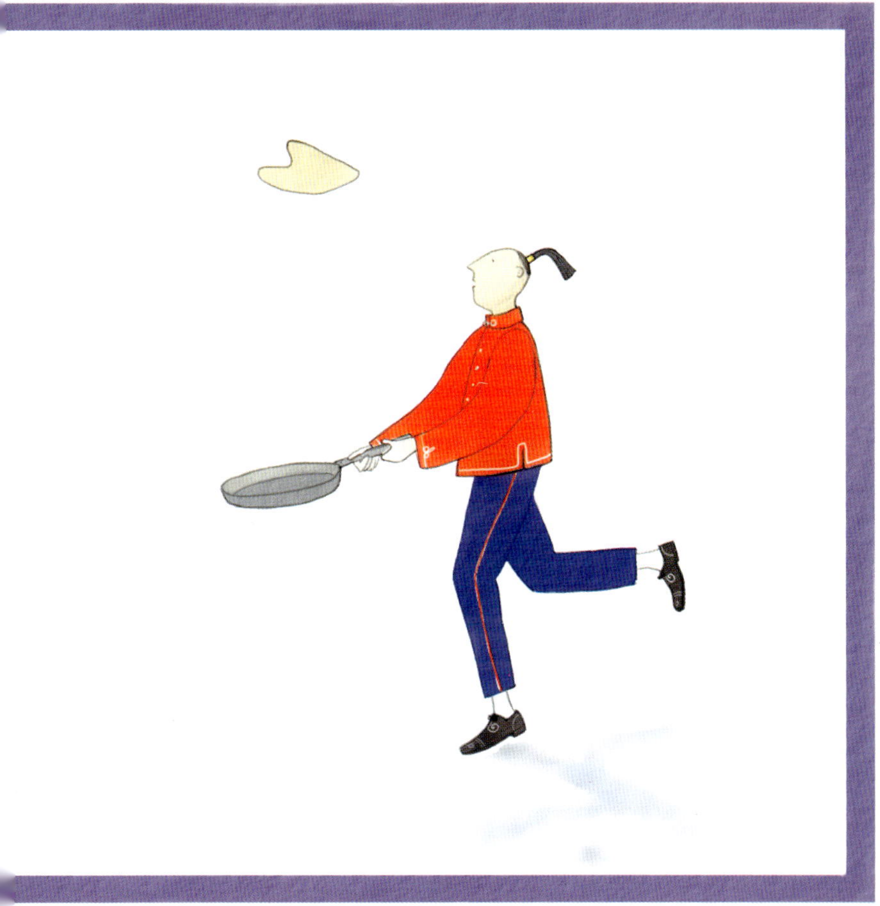

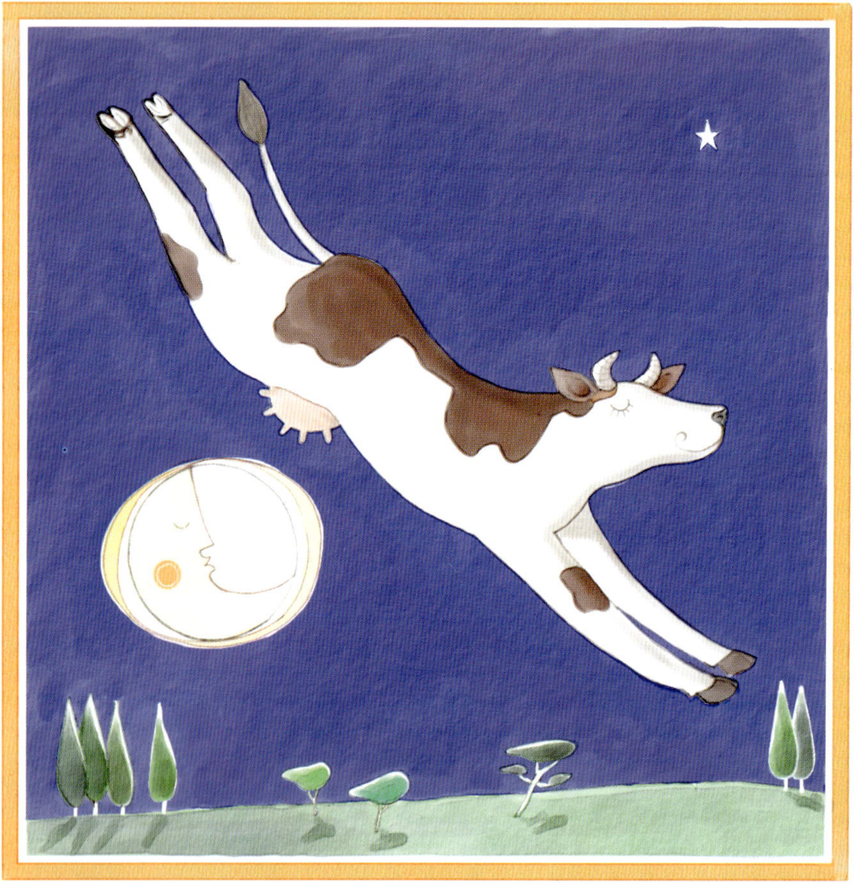

you send me over the
moon and happily
beyond reason

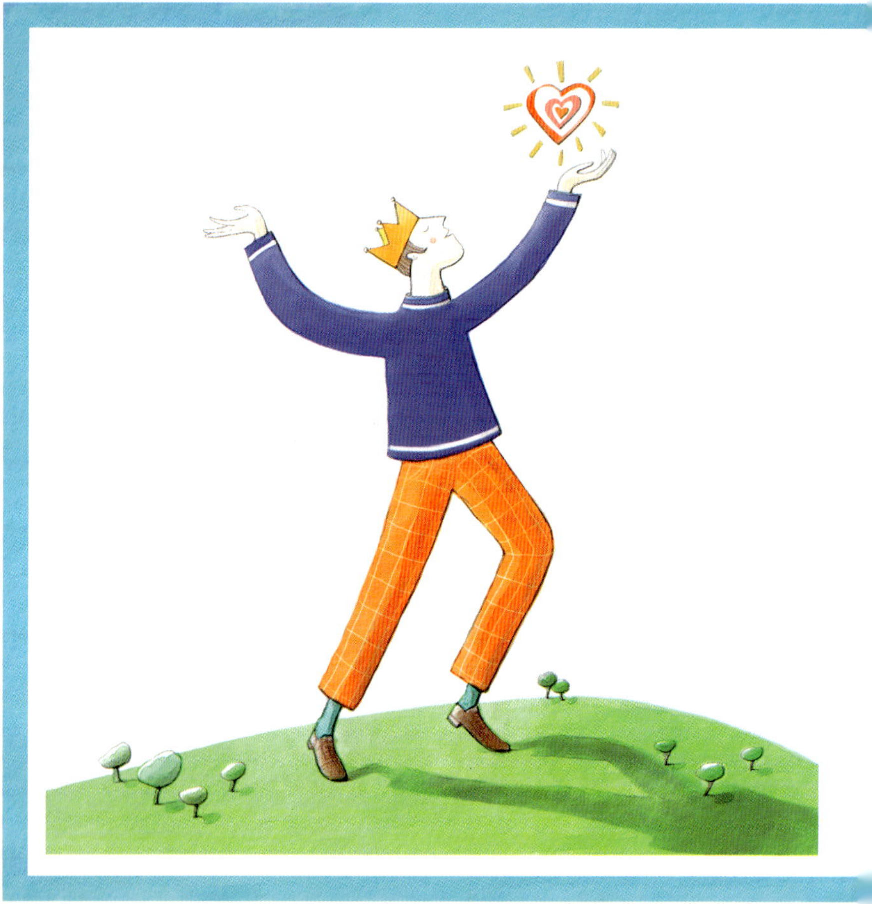

your love takes me

to the top of world

with you, I'm on cloud nine

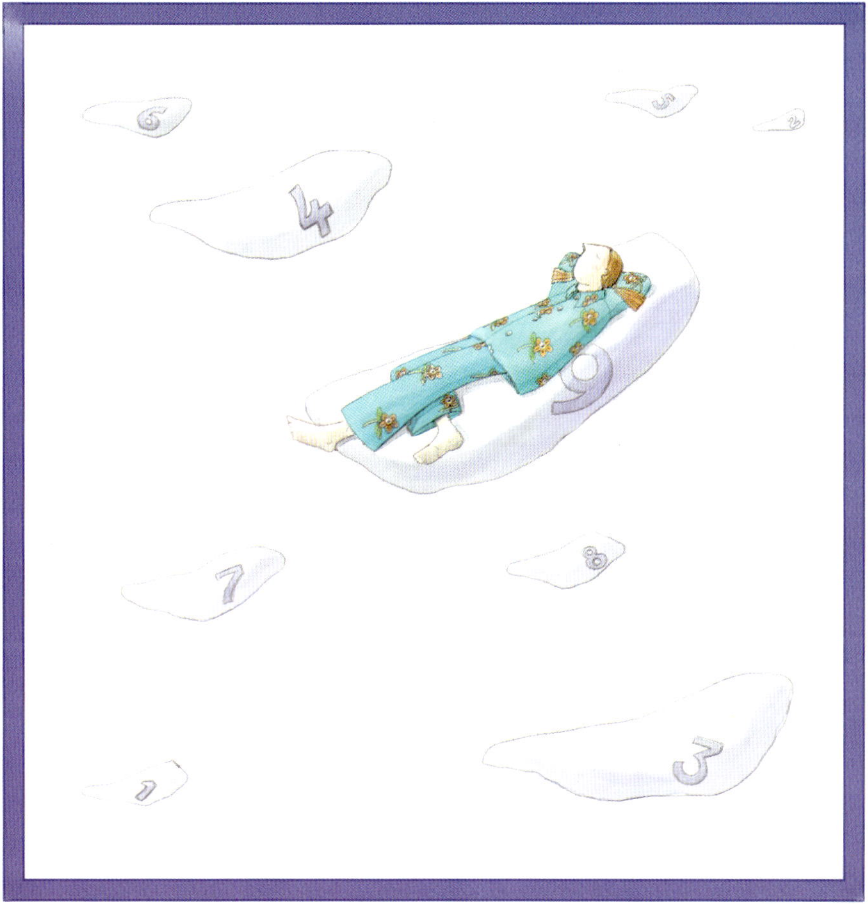
6
5
2
4
9
7
8
1
3

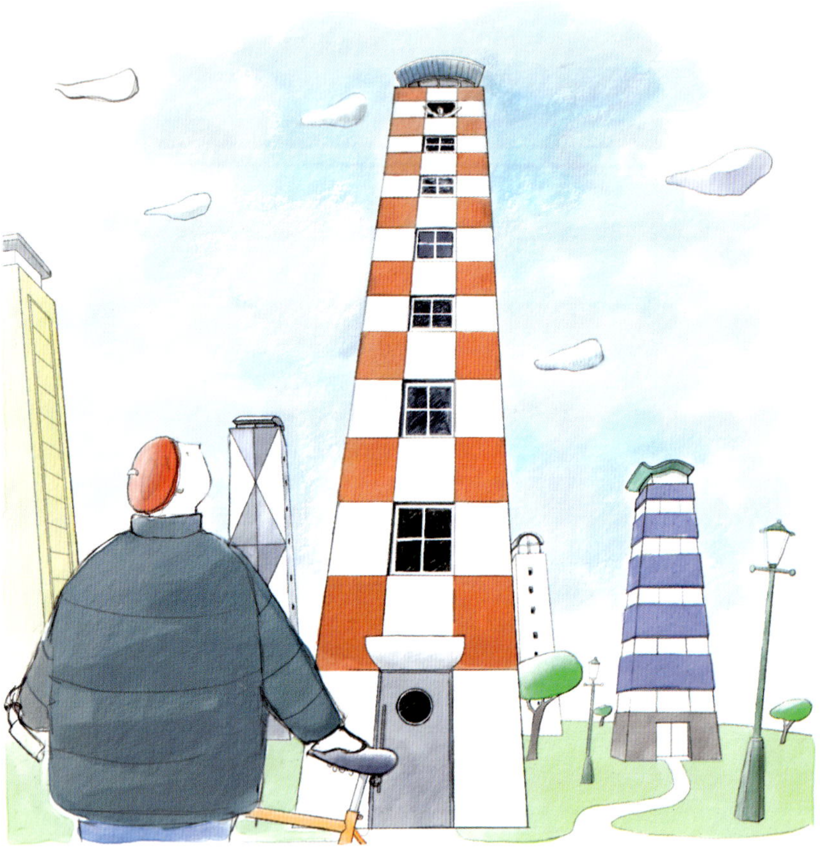

you make me feel like
singing out loud

Confetti Moment

★ 4 ★

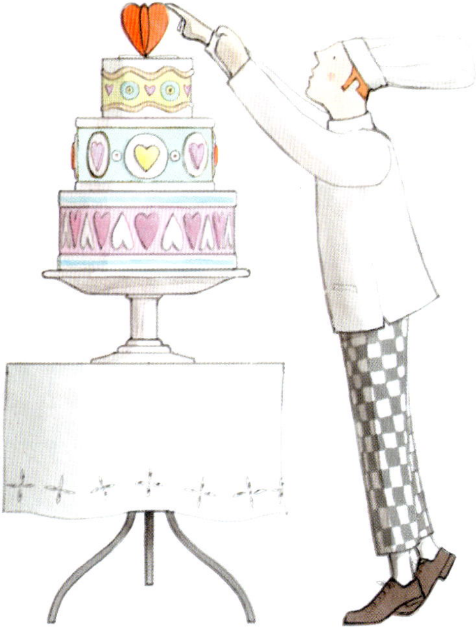

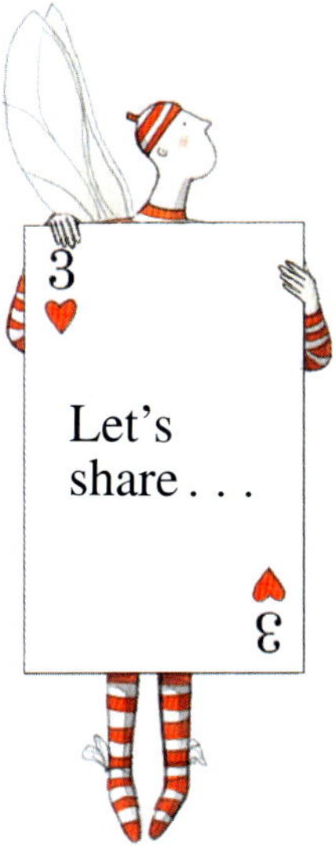
3
Let's share . . .
3

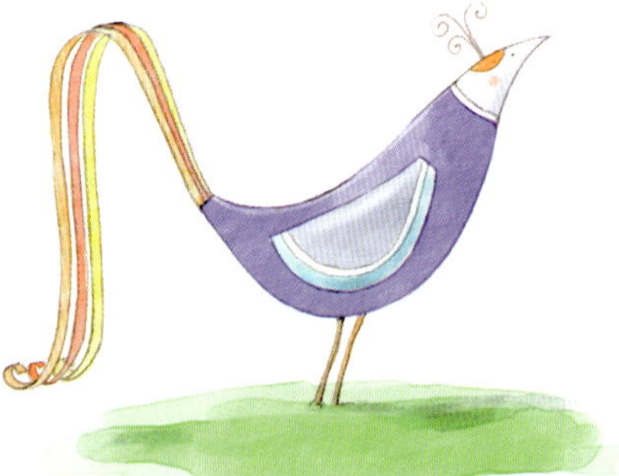

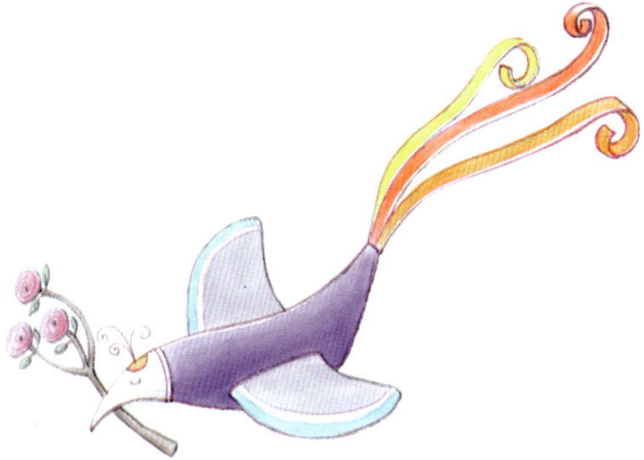

I bring you
my hopes
my dreams
and yes
my love

two lovebirds
two hearts
one promise

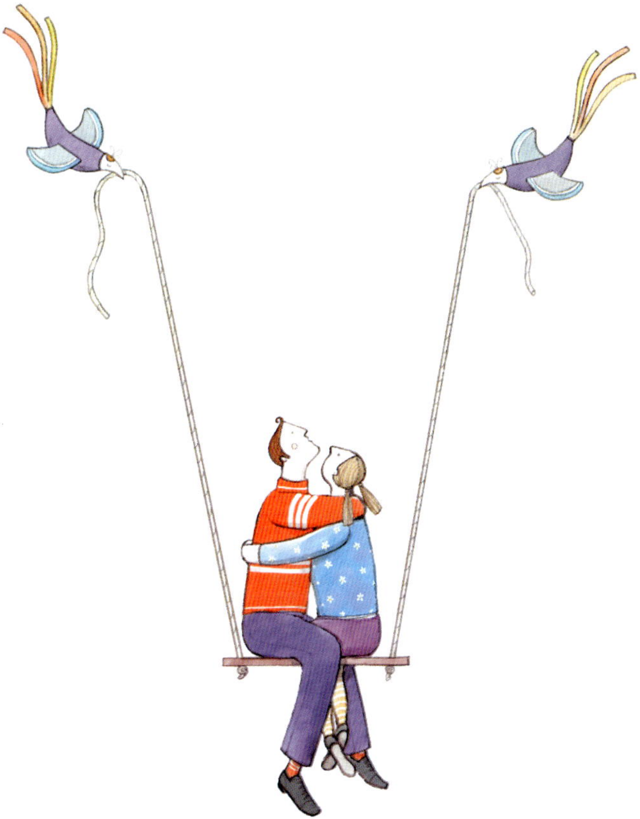

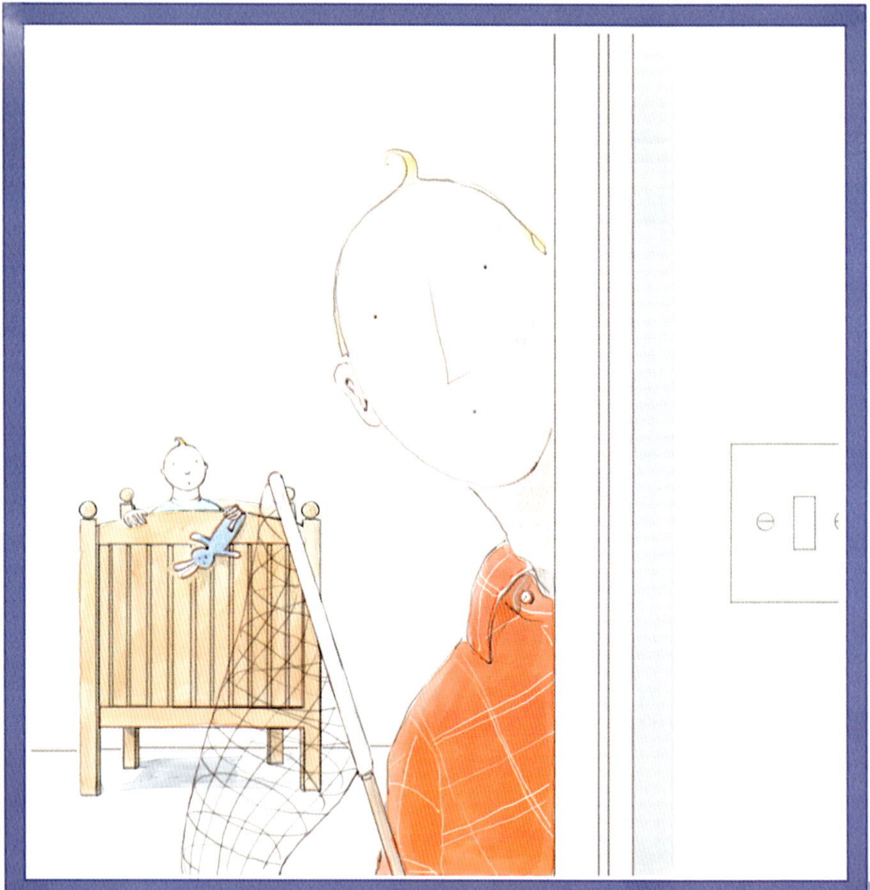

let me catch your bad dreams

CONFETTI MOMENT

★ 5 ★

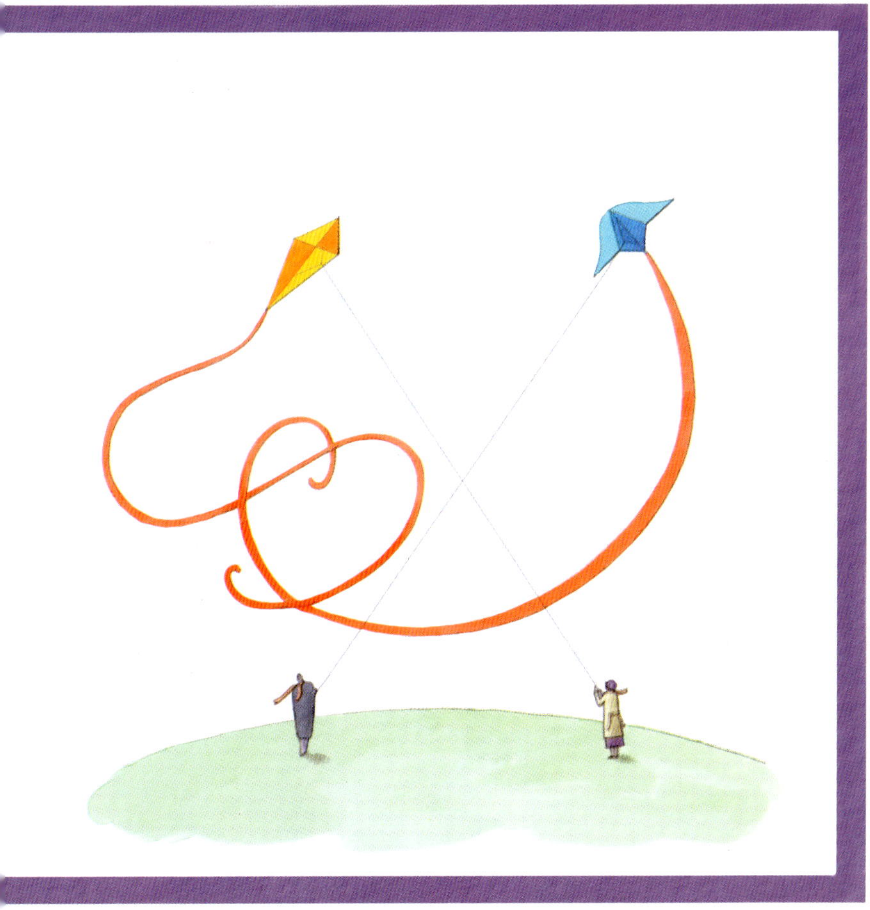

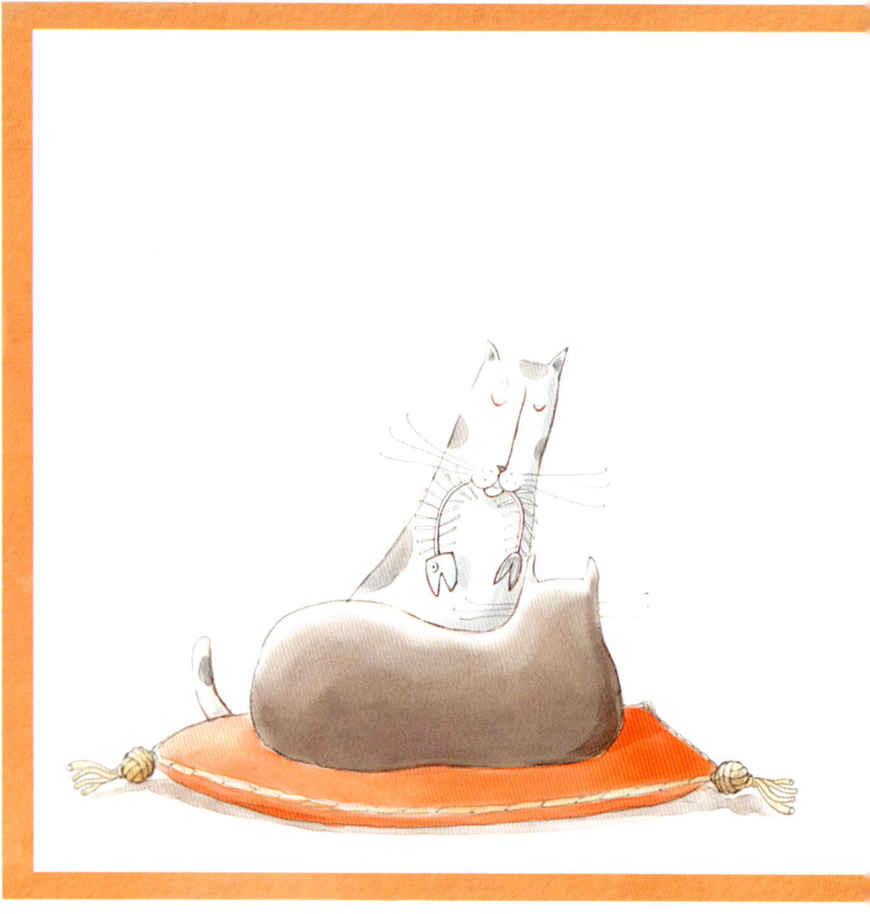

breakfast in bed?

your wish is my command

I love it when

you keep me warm

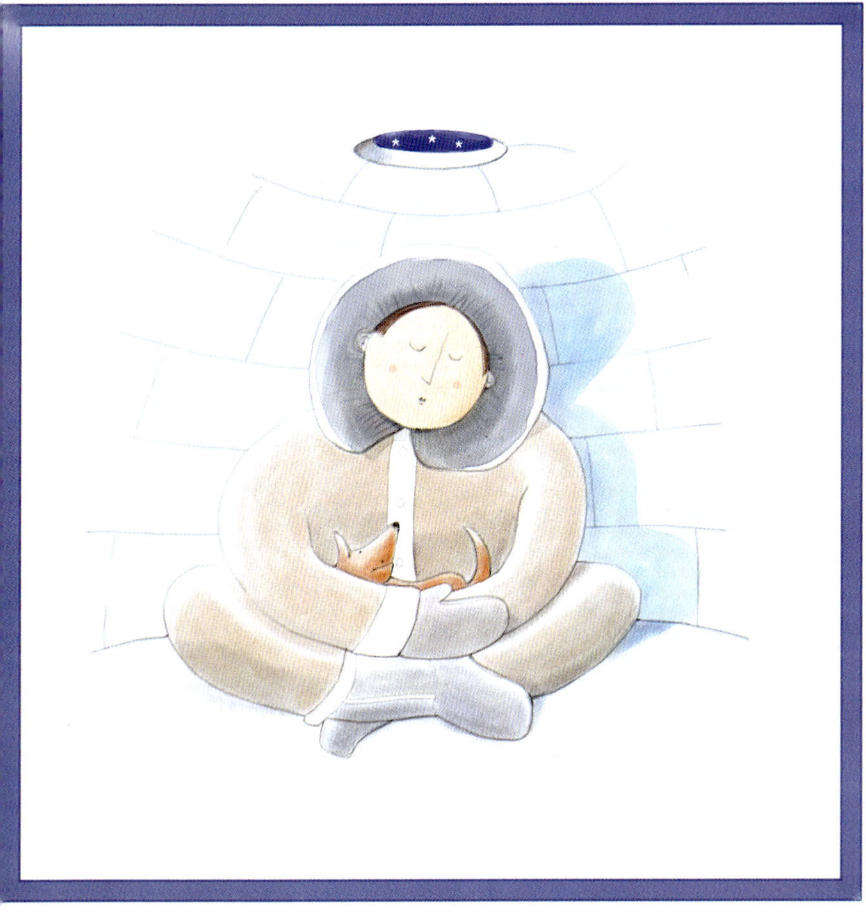

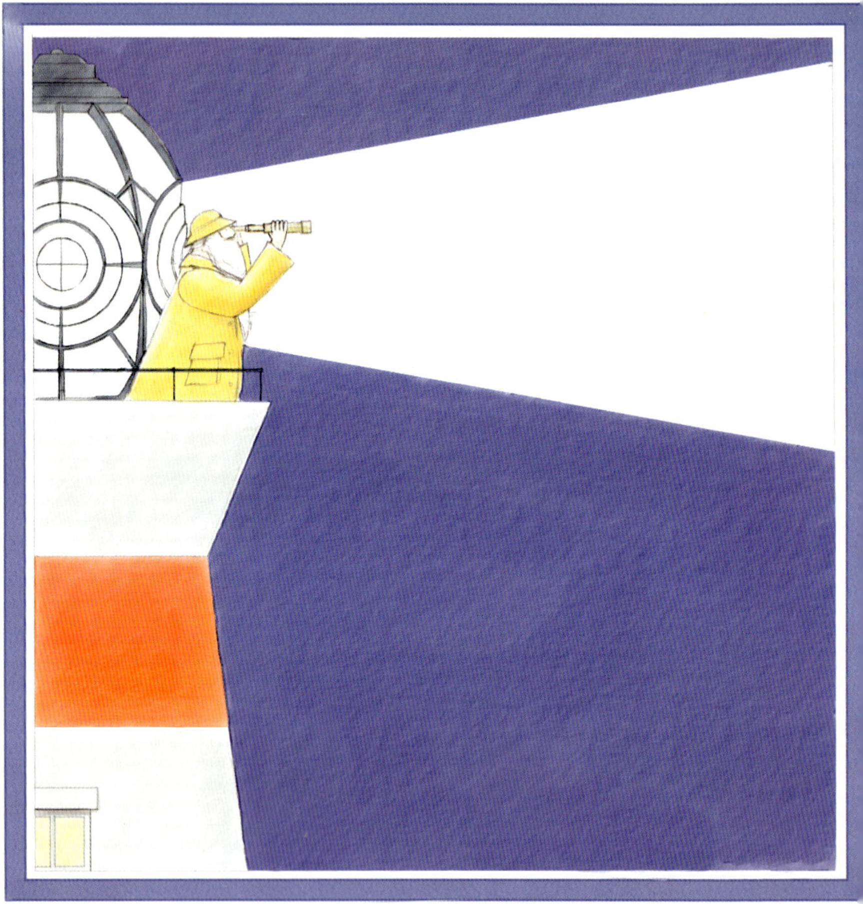

you always look out for me

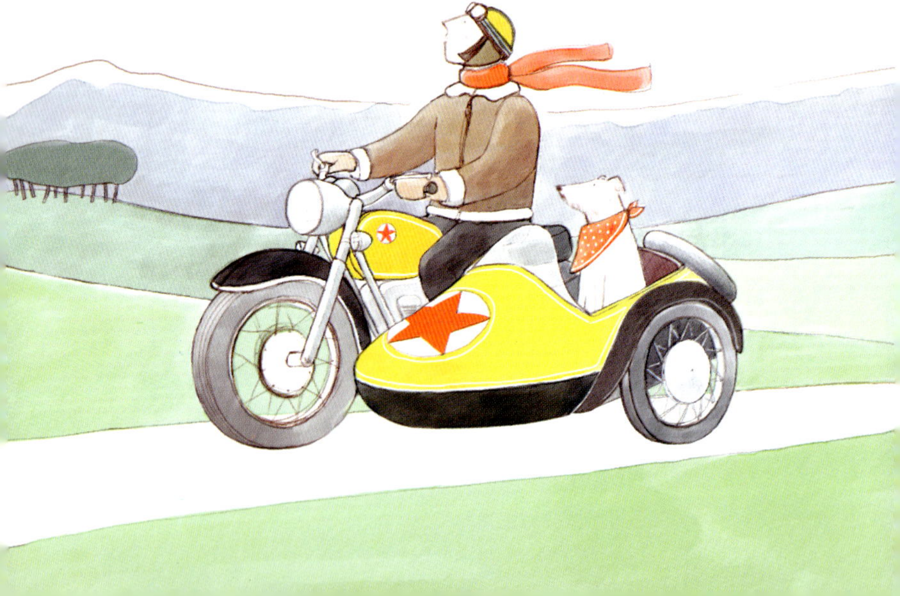

take me away from it all

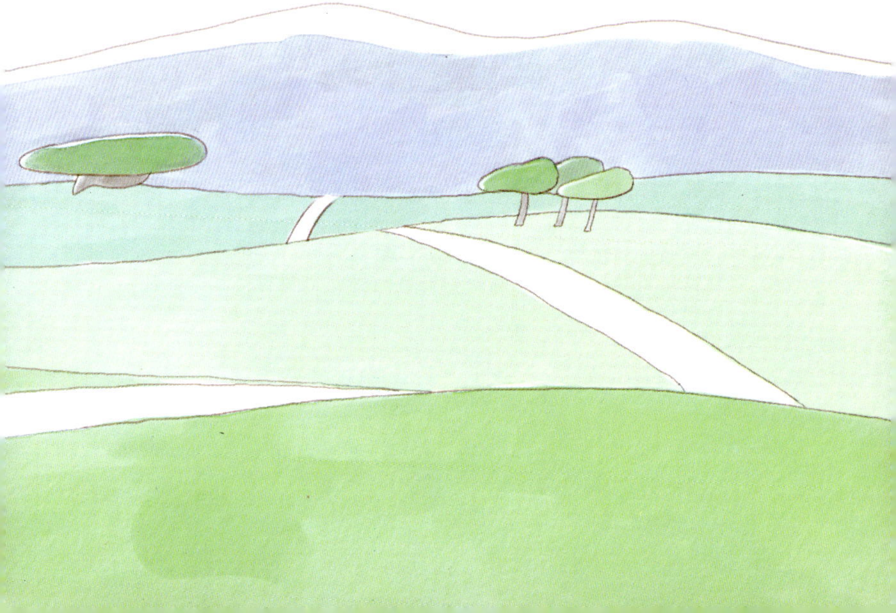

. . . my hero

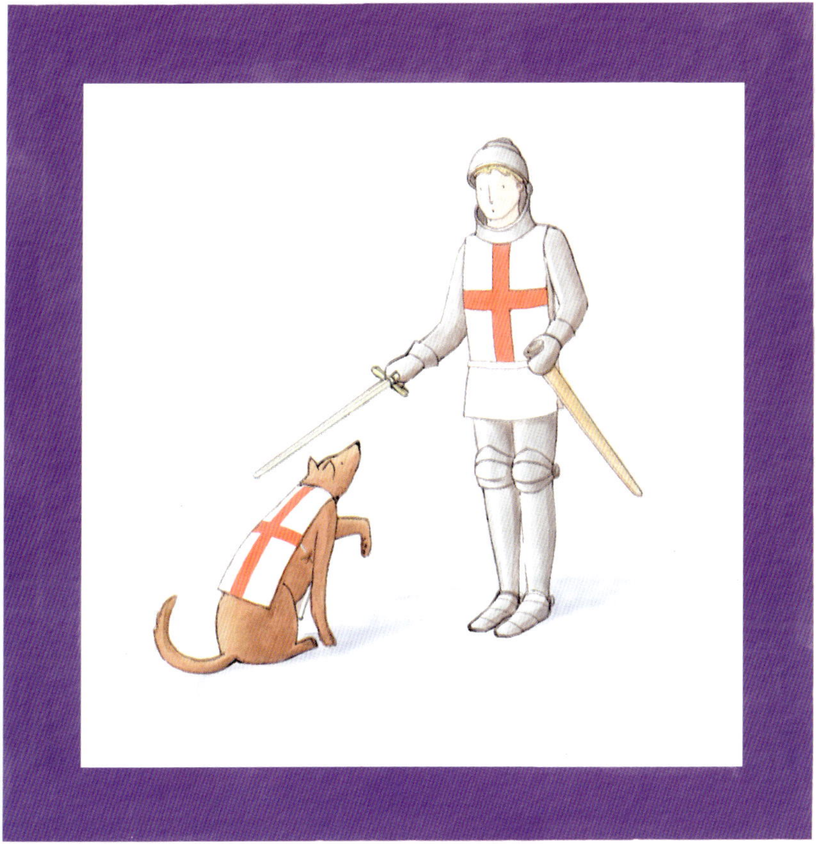

Confetti Moment

★ 6 ★

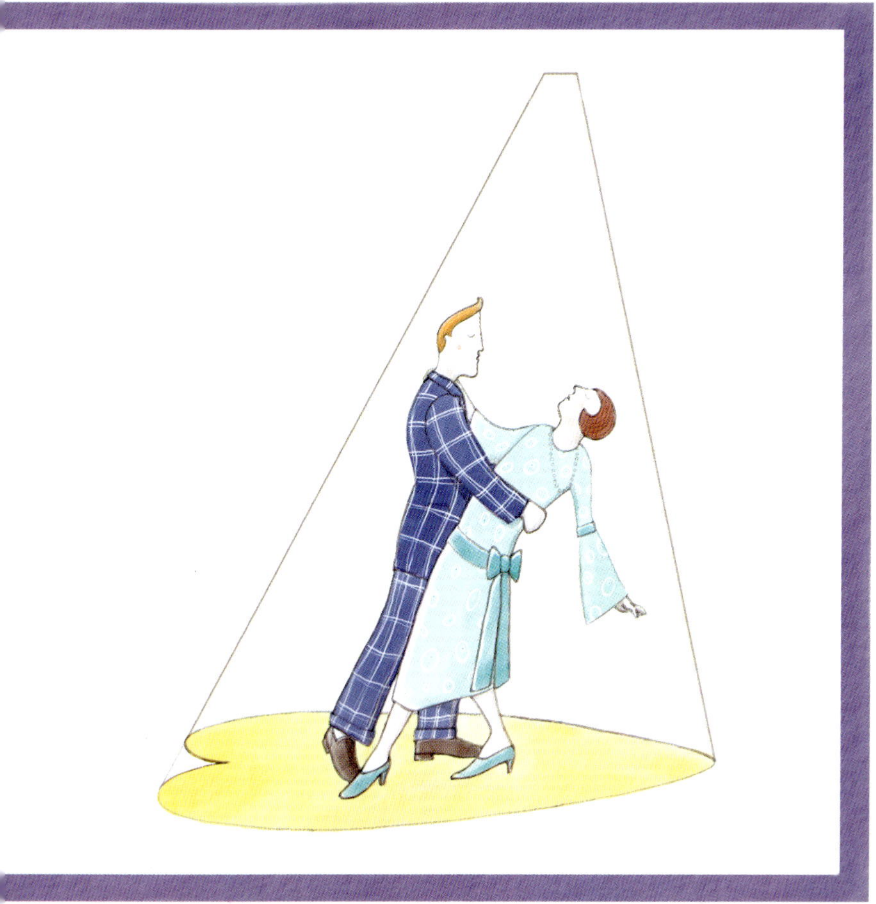

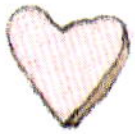

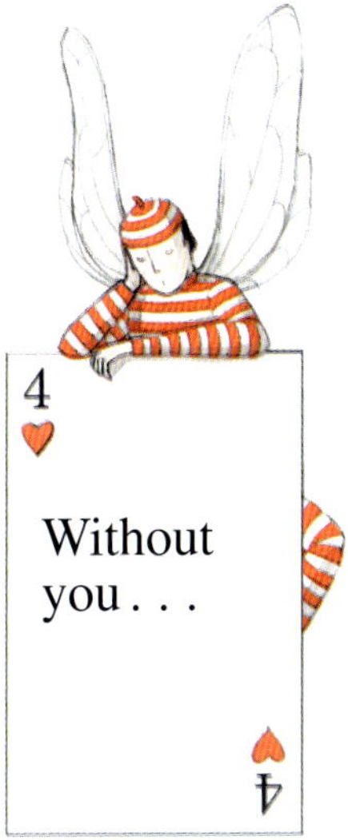
4
Without you . . .
4

no you

no love

no you

no heart

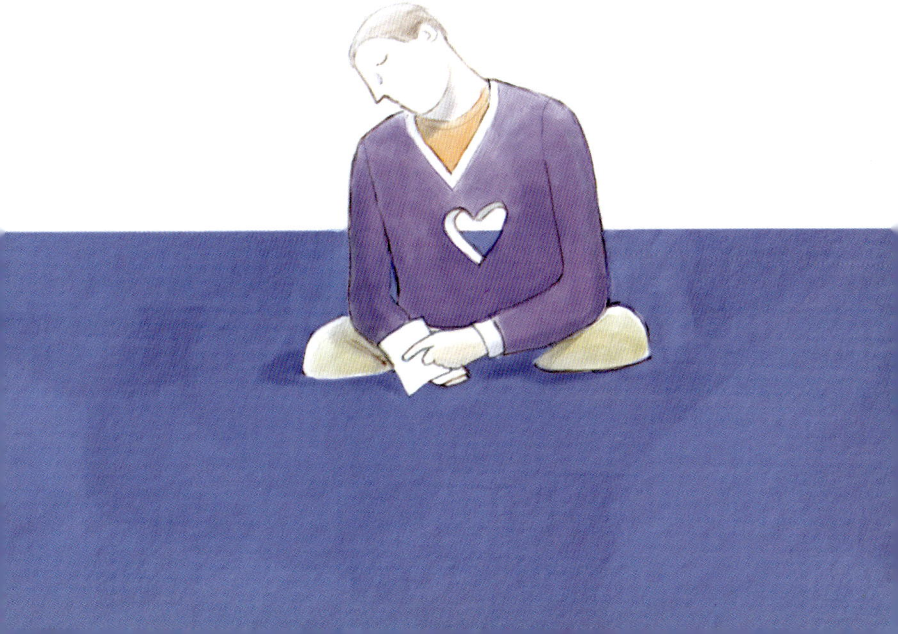

without you

I'm a party

waiting to happen

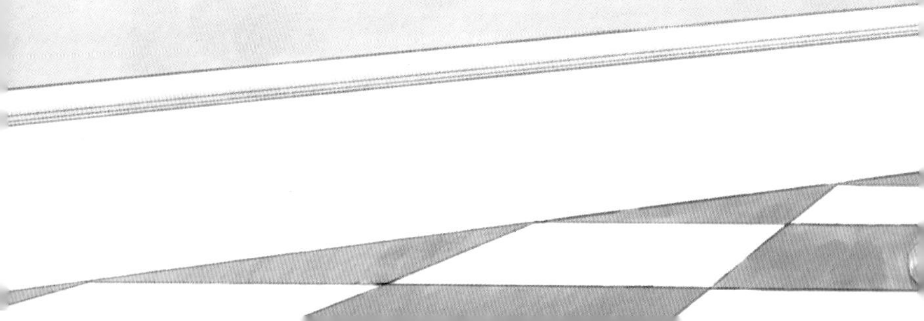

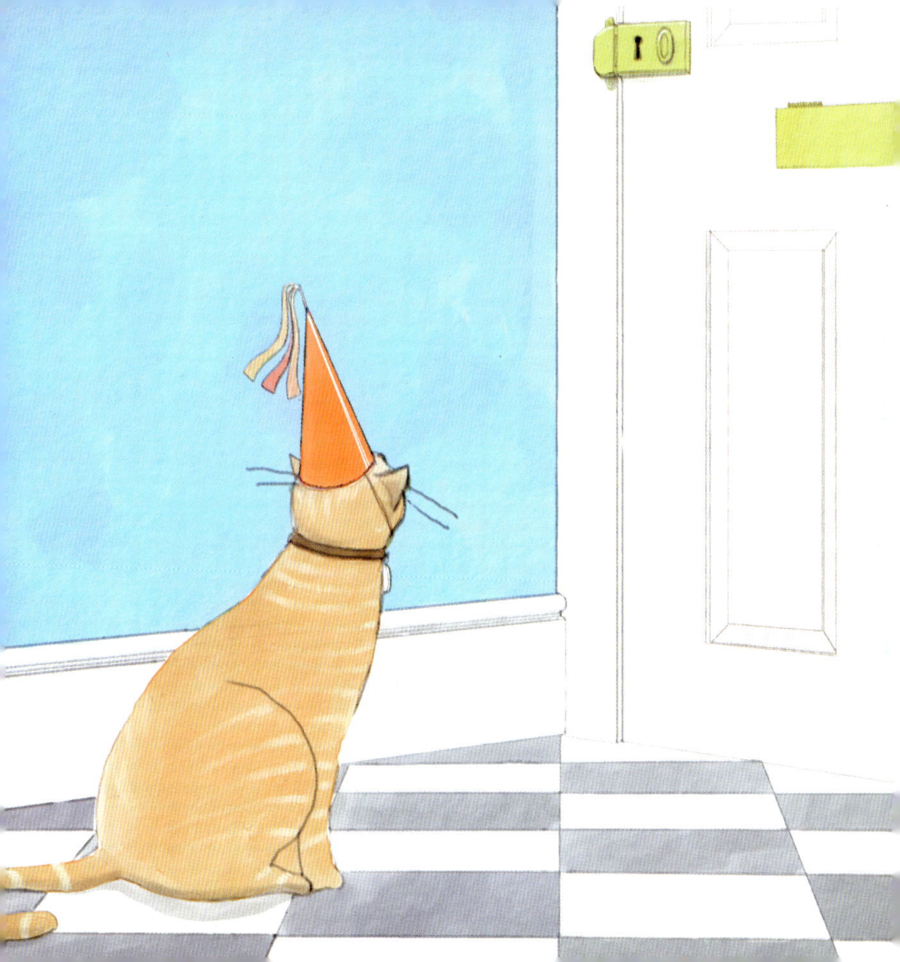

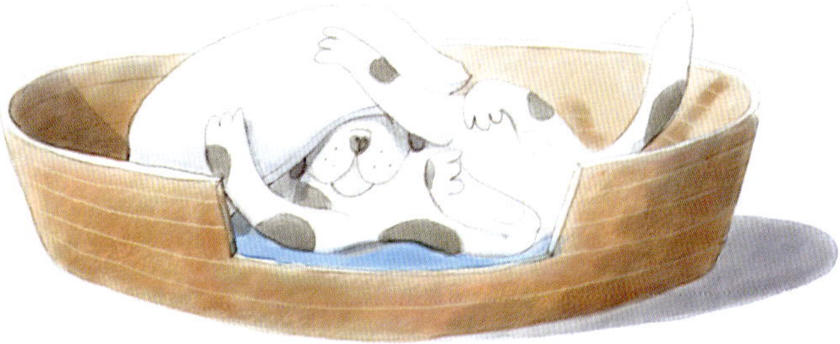

I can't face a day
without you

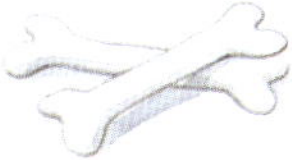

Confetti Moment

★ 7 ★

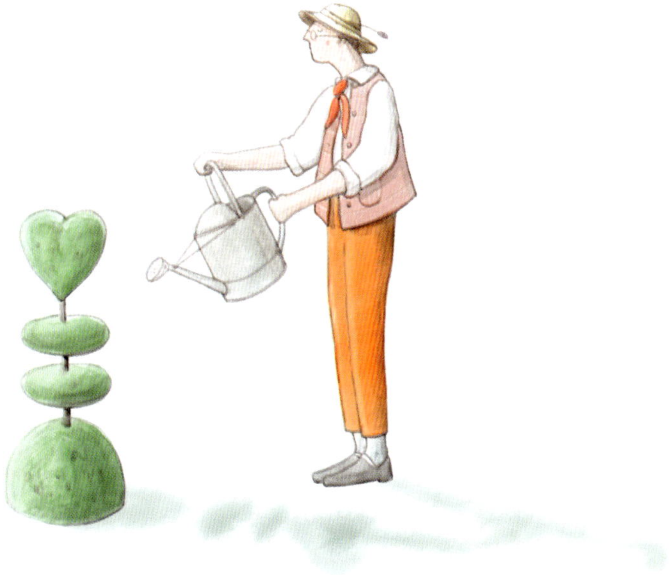

the bed's too big
without you

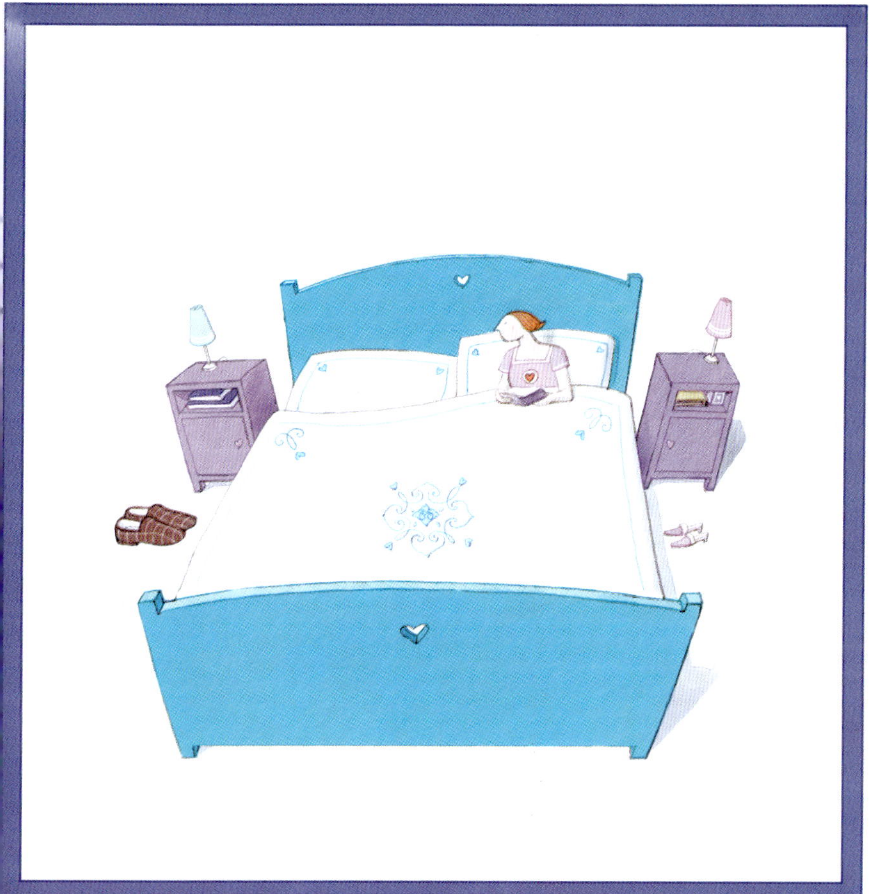

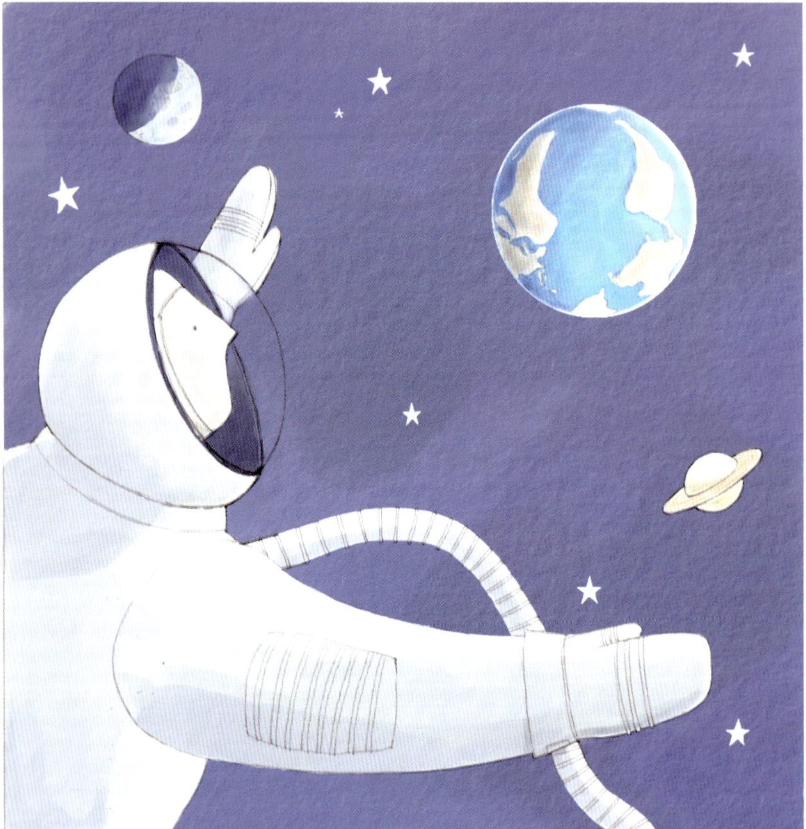

until you return

the minutes are light-years

and the world is

upside down

without you . . .

totally *blue*

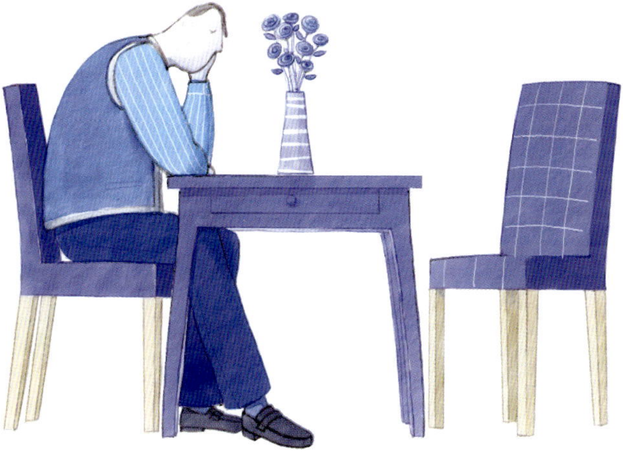

without you
the stars disappear
and even the moon is
all alone

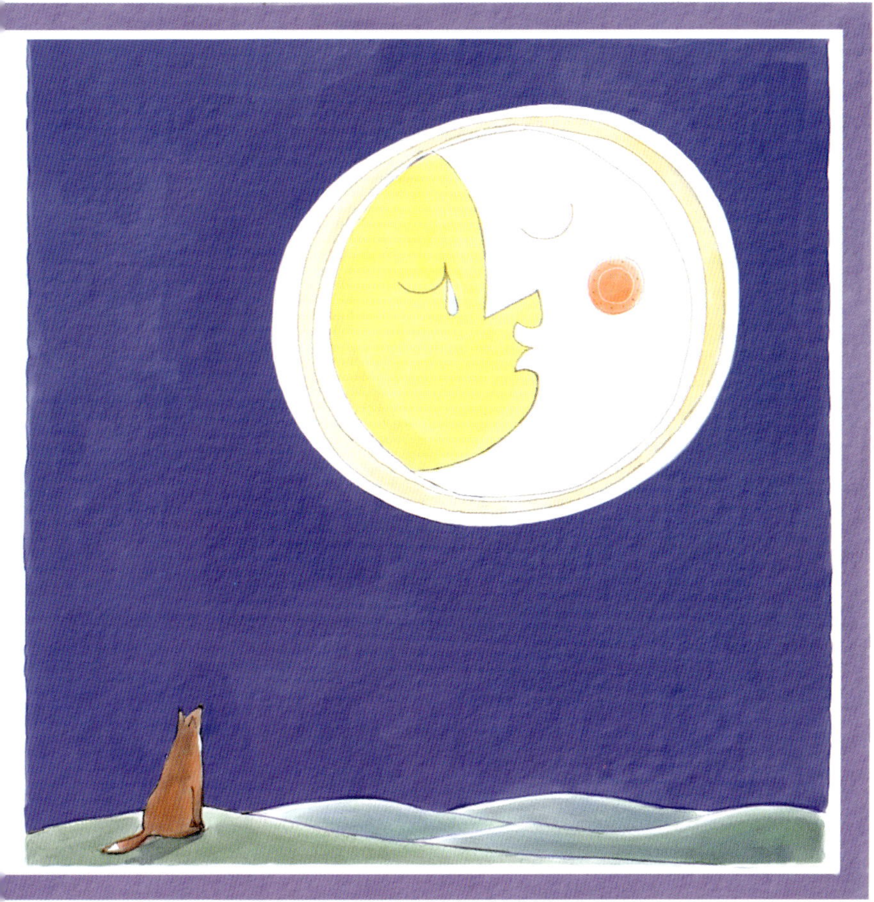

when you're not

around . . .

there's a dark cloud

everywhere

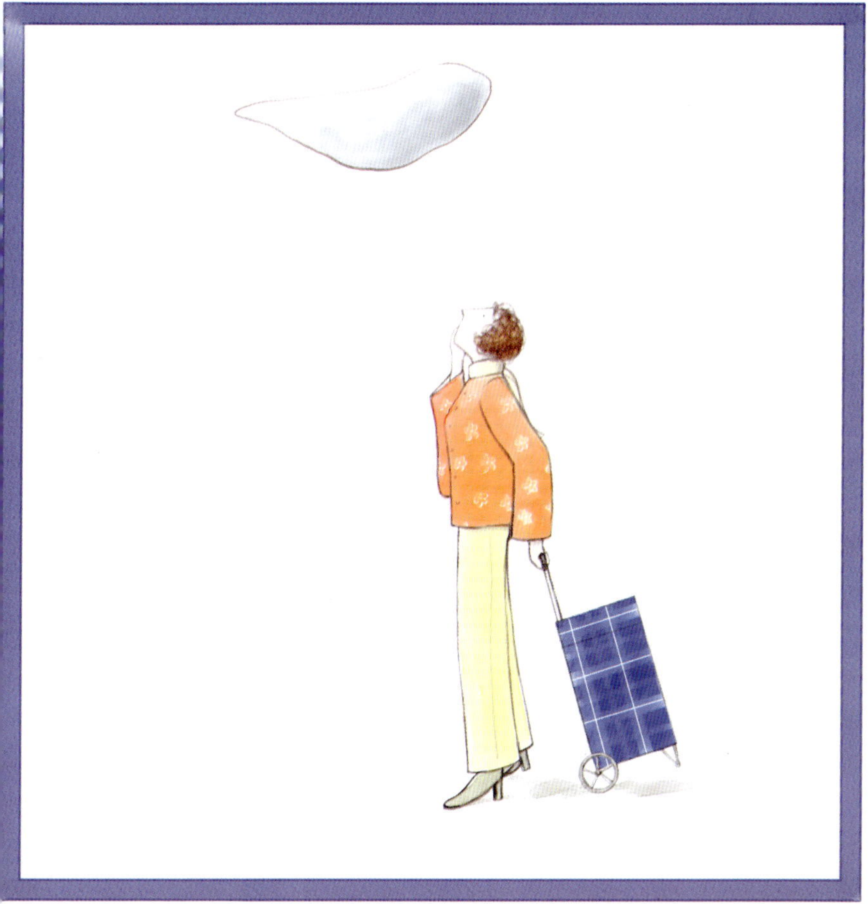

Confetti Moment

★ 8 ★

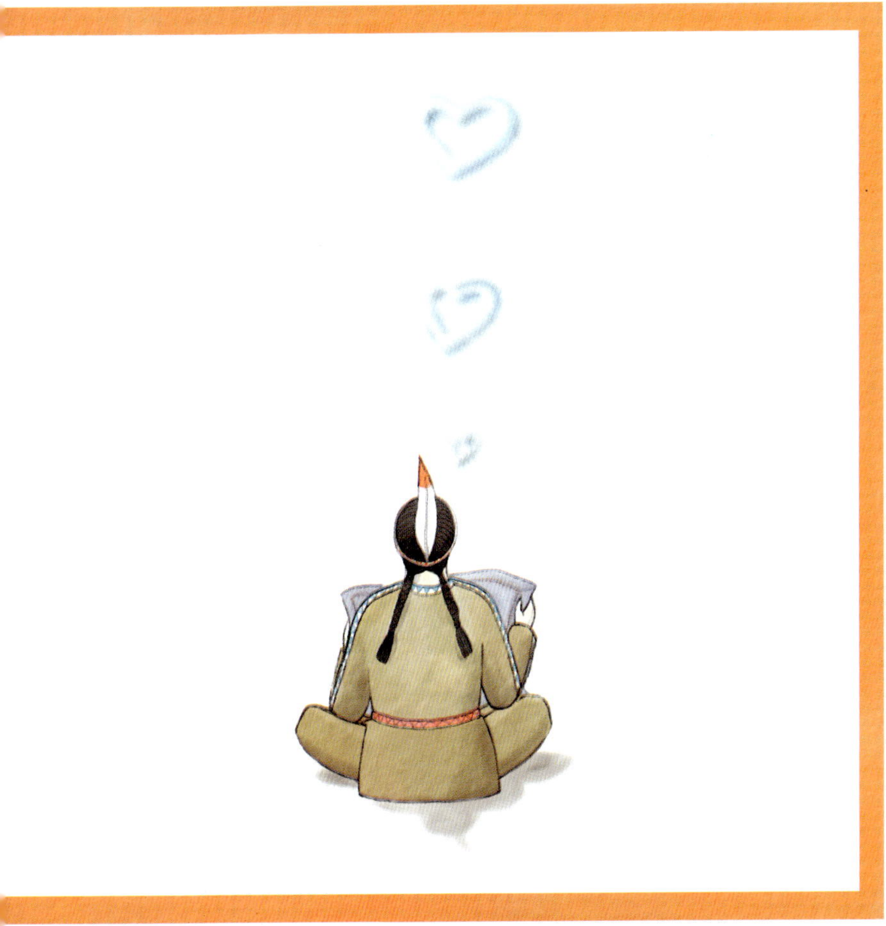

5
Our love is . . .
5

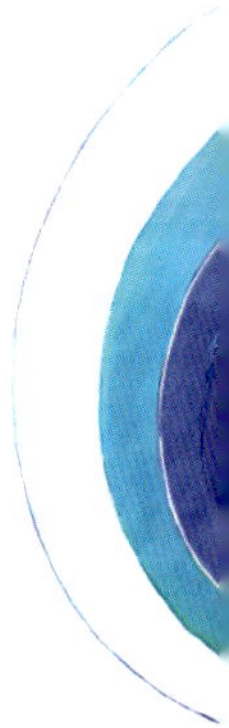

...a remarkable

force of nature

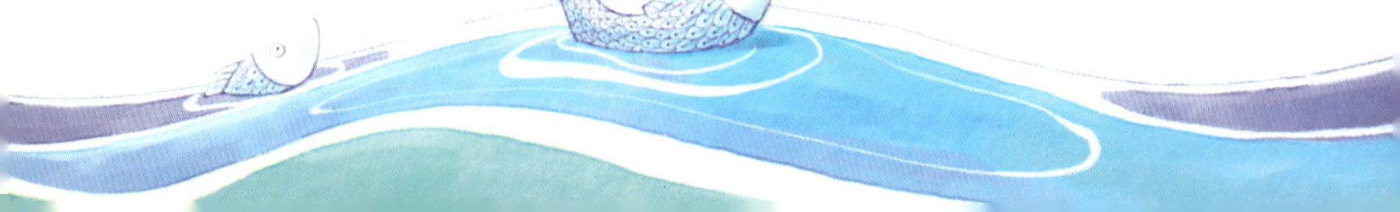

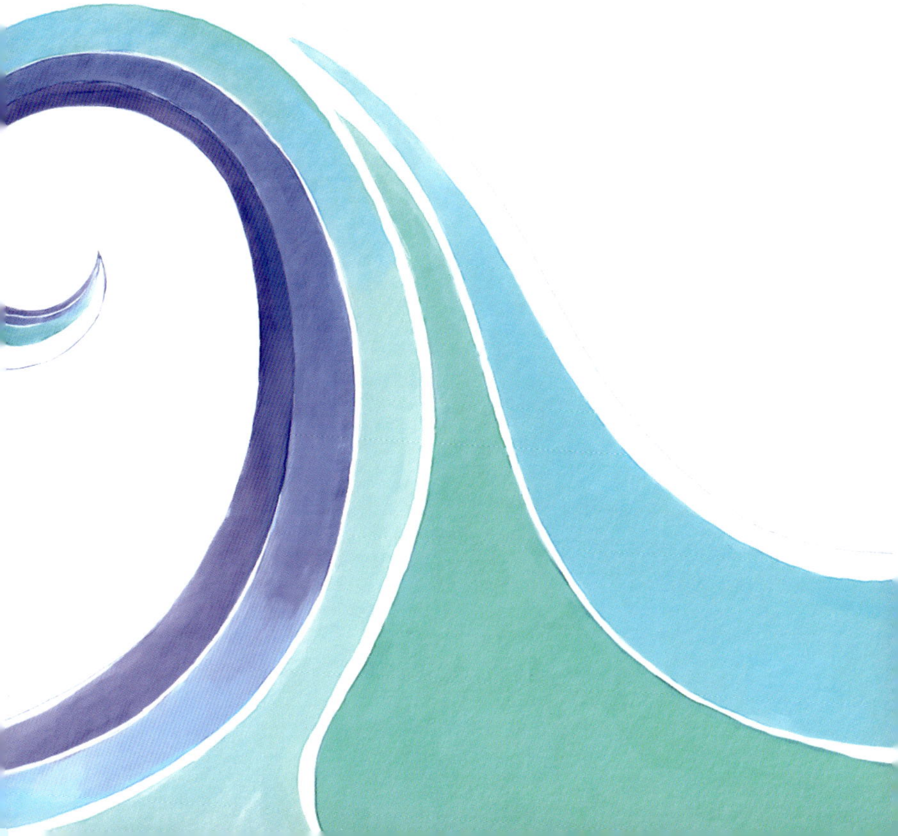

. . . as deep as

the old village well

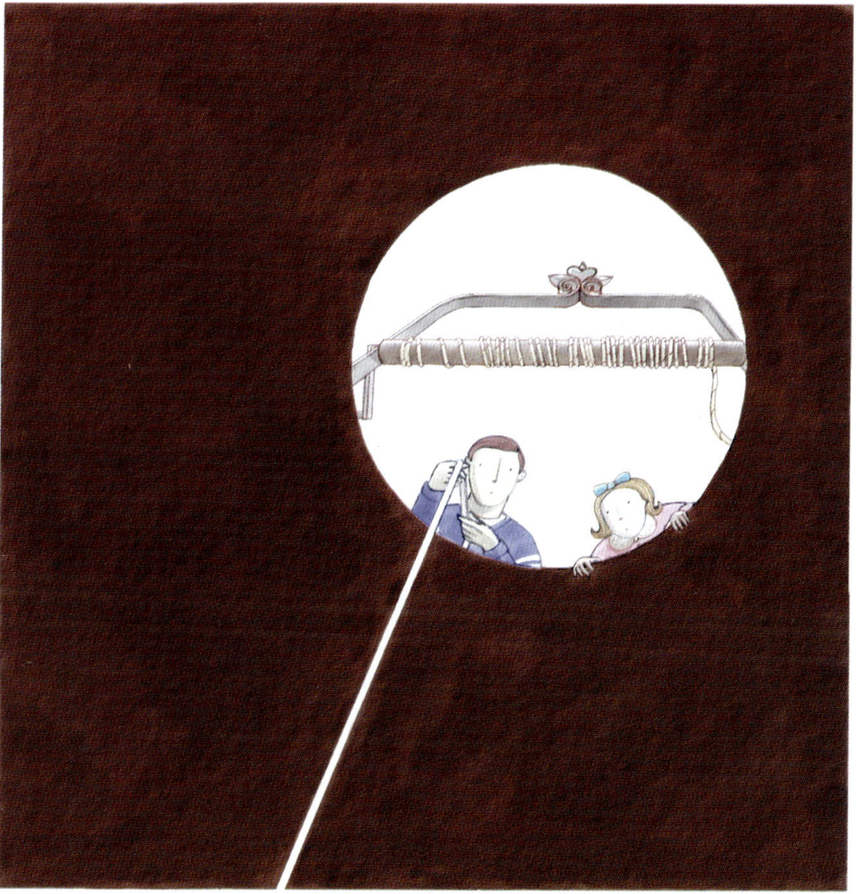

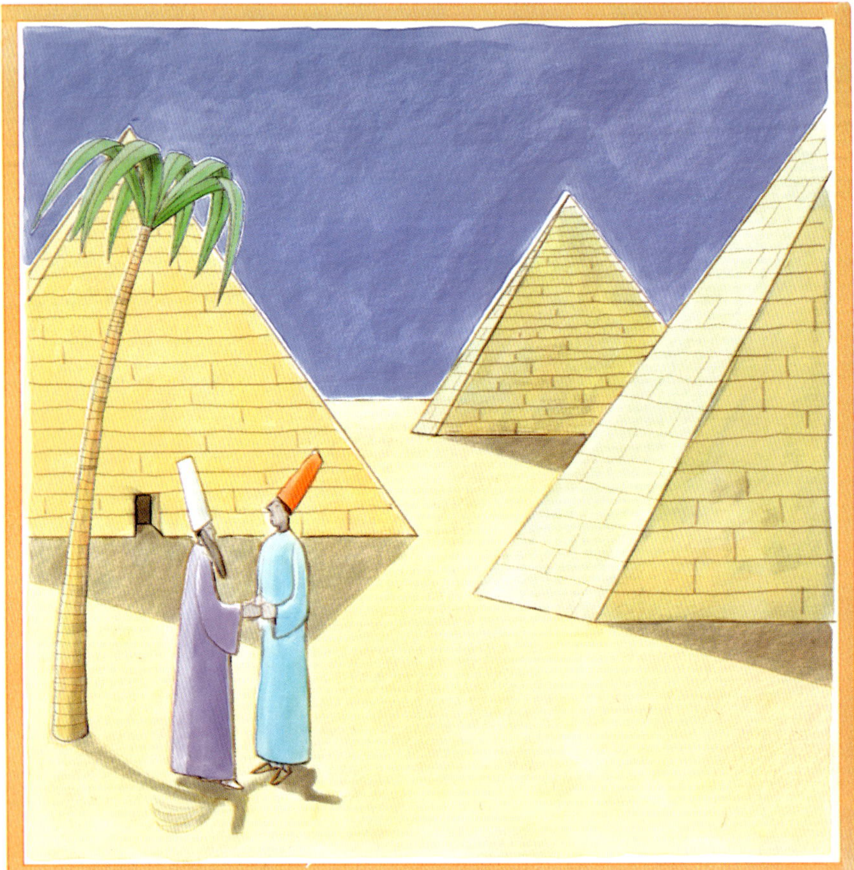

together we are timeless

CONFETTI MOMENT

★ 9 ★

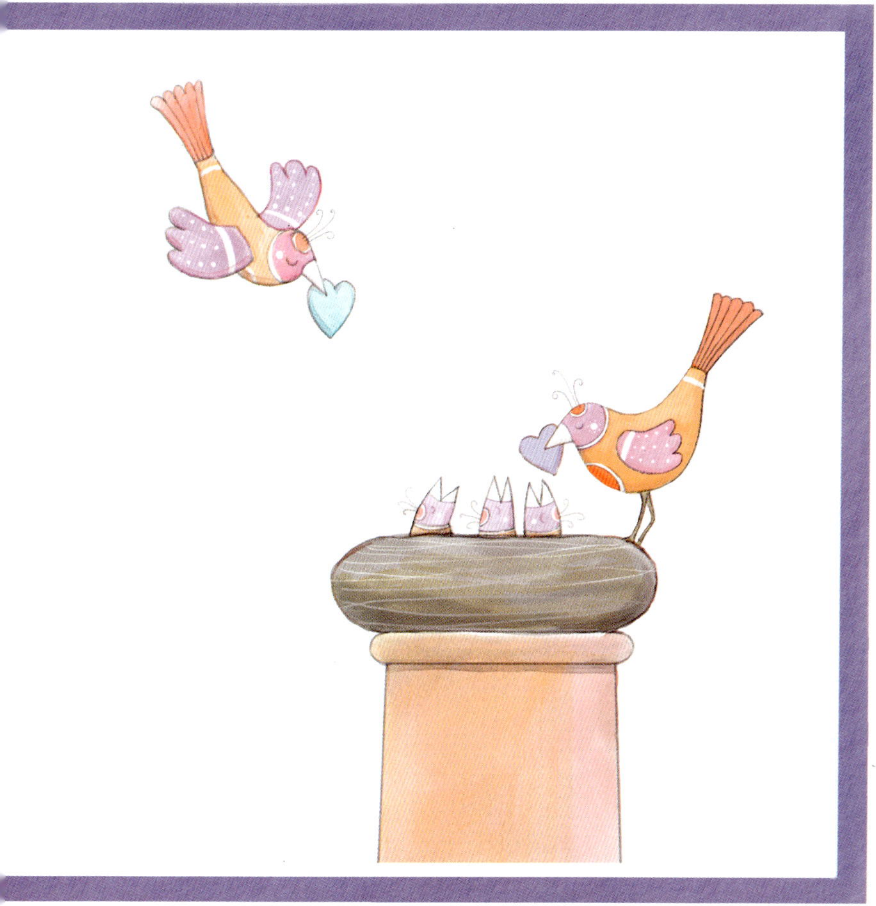

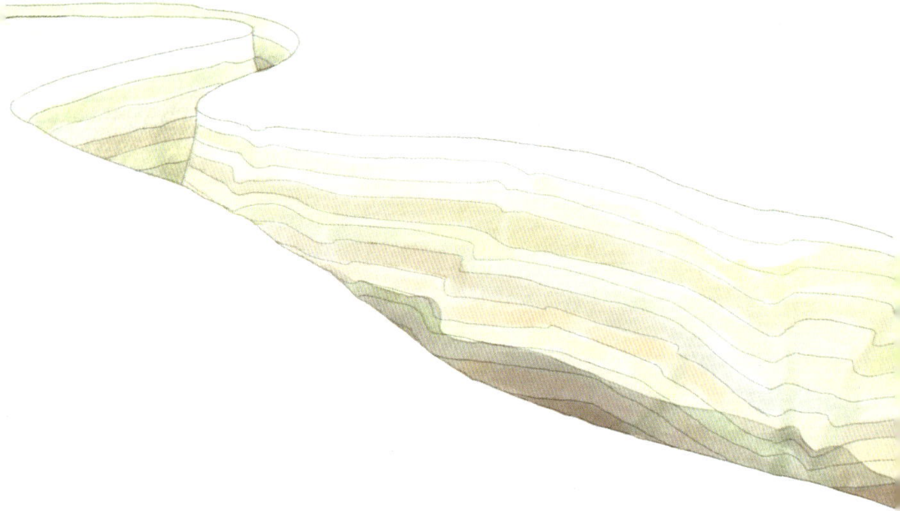

...another wonder

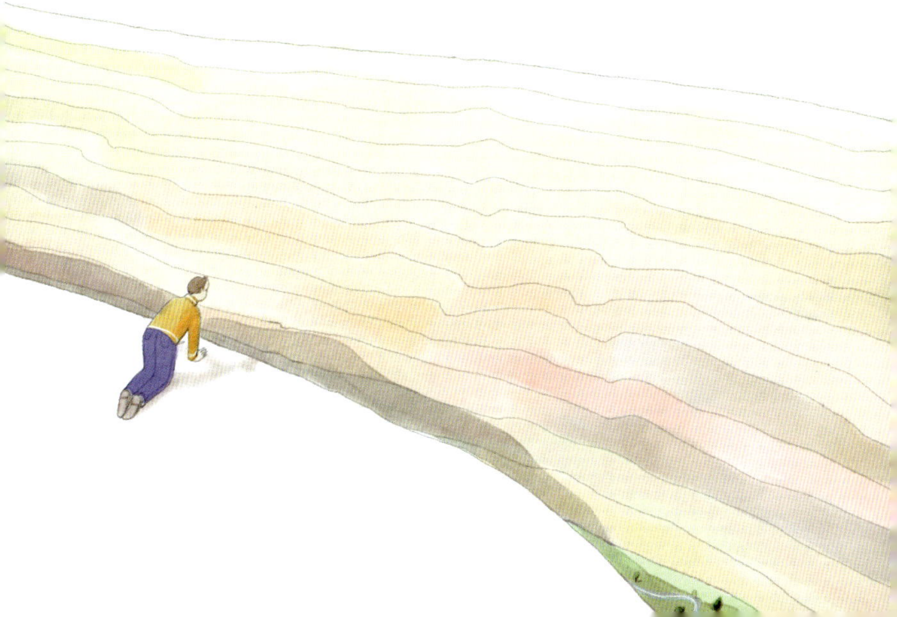

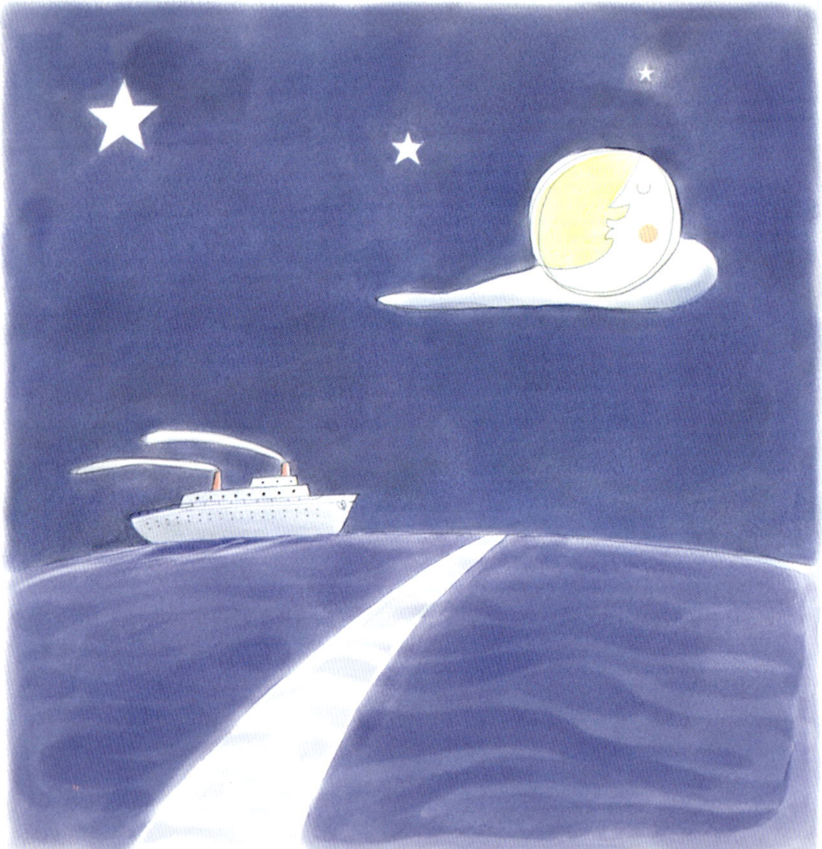

our love unfurls

like a ribbon

of moonlight

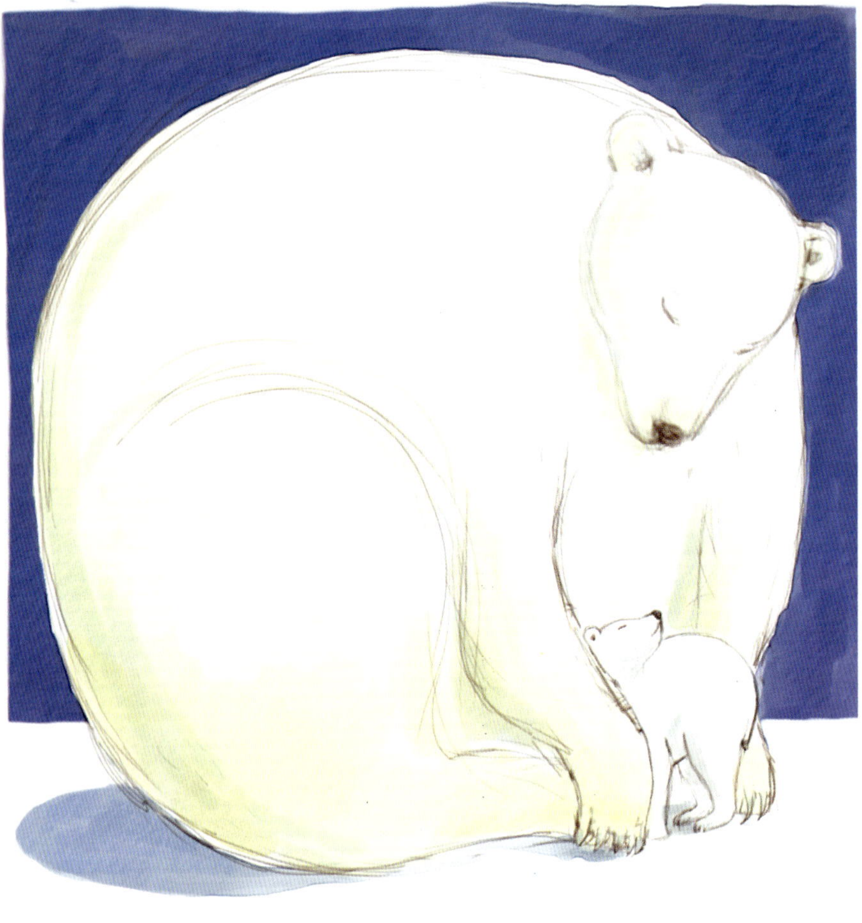

. . . a big bear hug

midnight skies
starlight sighs
and you

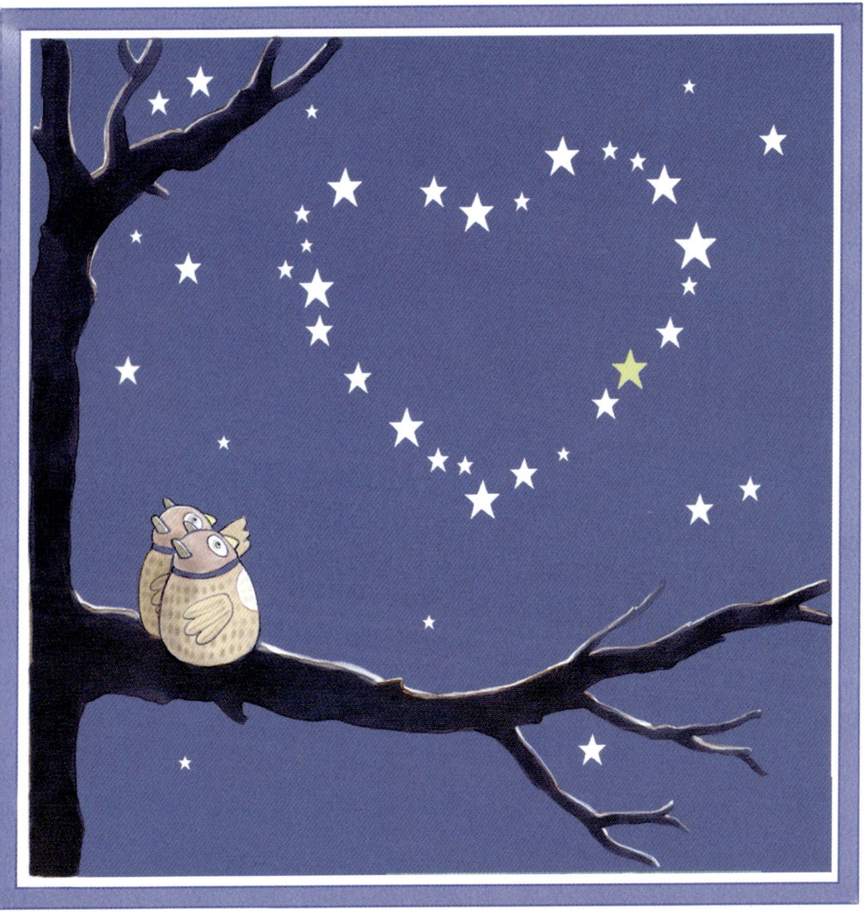

CONFETTI MOMENT

★ 10 ★

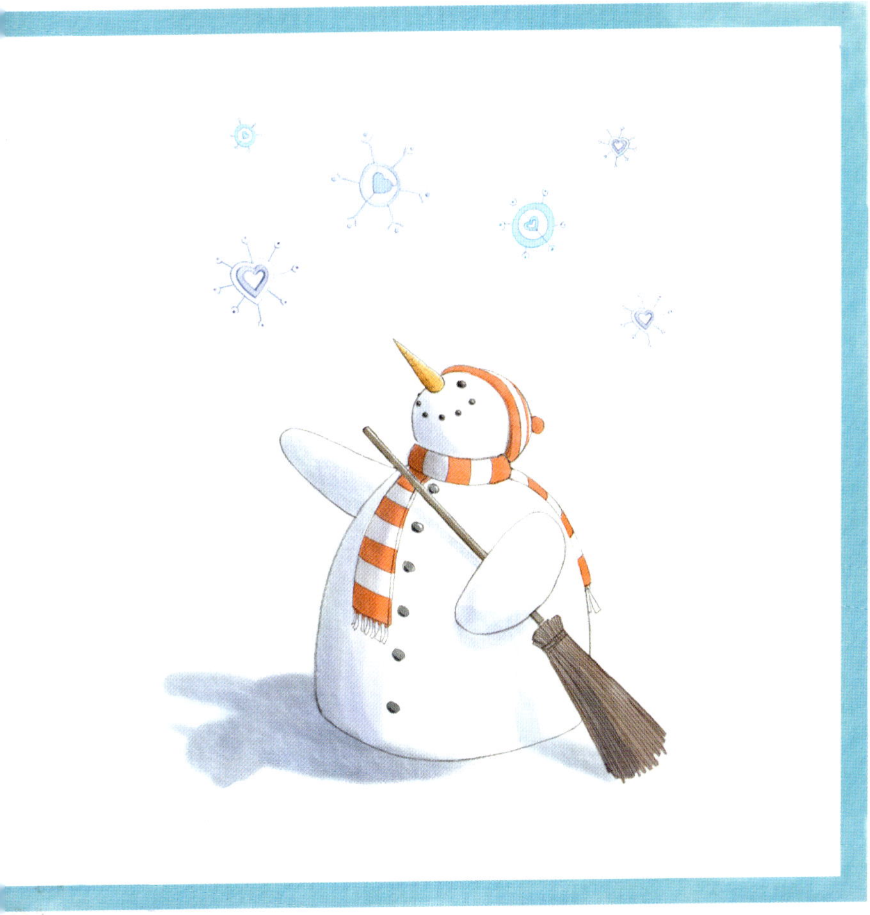

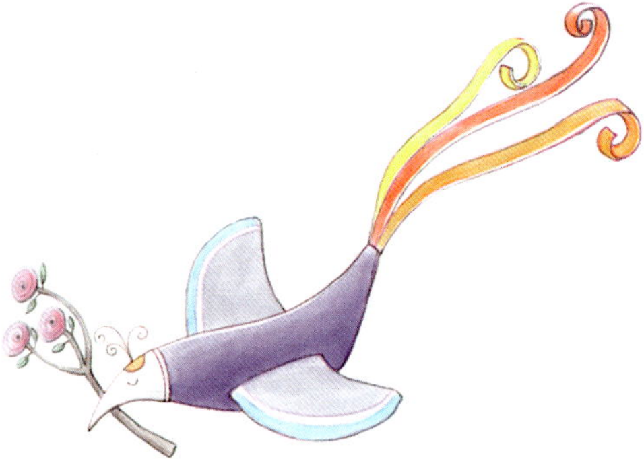

ABOUT THE ARTIST

Julia Glynn Smith worked as an architect and designer before illustrating her first book. She lives in Islington, London, but is never happier than when stepping out with a new map in hand and new places to discover.

First published by MQ Publications Limited
254–258 Goswell Road, London EC1V 7RL

ISBN: 0-7407-0550-4

Library of Congress Catalog Card Number: 99-67127

3 5 7 9 0 8 6 4 2

Printed and bound in China